This book is a gift from
Stafford County (Va) Chapter
of Chums, Inc.

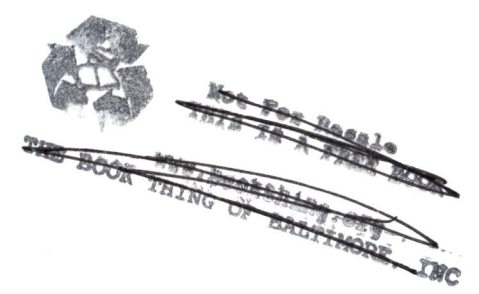

## INSECTS
### UNDER THE MICROSCOPE

# ON THE MOVE

CRAWLING, RUNNING, FLYING, AND LEAPING

First published in 2000 by
Grolier Educational
Sherman Turnpike
Danbury, Connecticut
© Quartz Editions 2000

All rights in this book are reserved. No part of this book may be used or reproduced in any manner whatsoever or transmitted in any form or by any means, electronic or mechanical, including photocopying, recording, or any information storage and retrieval system, without written permission of the copyright owner except in the case of brief quotations embodied in critical articles and reviews. For information, address the publishers:
Grolier Educational, Sherman Turnpike, Danbury, Connecticut 06816.

Library of Congress Cataloging-in-Publication Data

Under the microscope. Insects.
    p. cm.
   Includes indexes.
   Contents: v. 1. Lifecycles -- v. 2. Bodywork -- v. 3. On the move -- v. 4. Habitats -- v. 5. Record breakers -- v. 6 Behavior -- v. 7. Homes -- v. 8. Around people.
   ISBN 0-7172-9428-5 (set : alk. paper) -- ISBN 0-7172-9429-3 (v. 1 : alk. paper) -- ISBN 0-7172-9430-7 (v. 2 : alk. paper) -- ISBN 0-7172-9431-5 (vol. 3 : alk. paper) -- ISBN 0-7172-9432-3 (v. 4: alk. paper) -- ISBN 0-7172-9433-1 (v. 5 : alk. paper) -- ISBN 0-7172-9434-X (v. 6 : alk. paper) -- ISBN 0-7172-9435-8 (v. 7 : alk. paper) -- ISBN 0-7172-9436-6 (v. 8 : alk. paper)
   1. Insects -- Juvenile literature. [1, Insects.] I. Title: Insects. II. Grolier Educational (Firm)

QL467.2.U53 1999
595.7 -dc21                                                              99-040208

**Produced by Quartz Editions**
**Premier House**
**112 Station Road**
**Edgware HA8 7BJ**
**UK**

EDITORIAL DIRECTOR: Joy Francis
CREATIVE DIRECTOR: Marilyn Franks
PRINCIPAL ILLUSTRATOR: Neil Lloyd
CONTRIBUTING ILLUSTRATORS: Jim Channell, Tony Gibbons
ADDITIONAL CONTRIBUTORS: Susan Bennet, Enid Broderick, Hayley Daniel, Susan Diamond, Frances Freedman, Jo Goldberg, Anne Johnson, Ellen Laarous, Erica Matlow, Laurence Pinkus, Guy Regev, Diane Rich, Arlene Seaton

The publishers gratefully acknowledge the kind assistance of Matthew Robertson, entomologist and previously keeper of insects at London and Bristol Zoos, with the planning and compilation of this set. The guidance of the Department of Entomology at the Natural History Museum, London, is also much appreciated.

Reprographics by Repro Multi-Warna, Indonesia
Printed in Hong Kong

## ACKNOWLEDGMENTS

The publishers wish to thank the following for supplying photographic images for this volume.

Page 8 NHPA/S.Dalton; p9tl,br NHPA/S.Dalton; p9tr,bl BC/K.Taylor; p10tl BC/K.Taylor; p10bl NHPA/S.Dalton; p11t SPL/Dr.J.Brackenbury; p12 BC/Dr.J.Brackenbury; p13t OSF/K.B.Sandved; p13c OSF/A.Shay; p13b BC/K.TayLor; p14t NHPA/S.Dalton; p14b BC/K.Taylor; p15t NHPA/G.I.Bernard; p15 BC/A.Purcell; p17bc BC/K.Taylor; p17r NHPA/S.Dalton; p18 BC/M.P.L.Fogden; p19c SPL/P.Menzel; p19b OSF/R.H.Kuiter; p20tl BC/Dr.F.Sauer; p20tr OSF/A.Shay; p20cl NHPA/S.Dalton; p21tr OSF/H.Fox; p21cr,br NHPA/S.Dalton; p22 SPL/C.Nuridsany & M.Perennou; p23t SPL/Dr.M.Read; p23c BC/G.Cubitt; p24tl OSF/P.O'Toolej p24cl OSF/B.Wells; p24b BC/C.C.Lockwood; p25tl OSF/R.Mayr; p26 BC/K.Taylor; p27tl OSF/C.Milkins; p27tr BC/K.Taylor; p27b SPL/ C.Nuridsany & M.Perennou; p28 NHPA/S.Dalton; p29tl SPL/K.H.Thomas; p29cr SPL/C.Nuridsany & M. Perennou; p30t,b NHPA/S.Dalton; p30cl,cr NHPA/ D.Heuclin; p32 BC/K.Taylor; p33 OSF/J.Mitchell; p34OSF/K.andved; p35tl OSF/H.Fox; p35tr BC/I.Arndt; p35b SPL/C.Nuridsany & M.Perennou; p36t,b NHPA/A.Bannister; p36c OSF/P.Devries; p38 SPL/Dr.M.Read; p39tr OSF/S.Camazine; p39br BC/K.Taylor; p41tl SPL/C.Nuridsany & M.Perennou; p41tr OSF/Animals,Animals; p41cr SPL; p41b BC/M.P.L.Fogden; p42t NHPA; p42b NHPA/O.Rogge; p43 NHPA/S.Dalton; p45tl SPL/J.Shemilt; p45bl NHPA/N.A.Callow; p45br NHPA/G.Bernard.

Abbreviations: Bruce Coleman (BC); Natural History Photographic Agency (NHPA); Oxford Scientific Films (OSF); Science Photo Library (SPL); bottom (b); center (c); left (l); right (r); top (t).

# INSECTS
## UNDER THE MICROSCOPE

# ON THE MOVE

### Crawling, Running, Flying, and Leaping

## GROLIER EDUCATIONAL
Sherman Turnpike, Danbury, Connecticut 06816

# ABOUT THIS BOOK

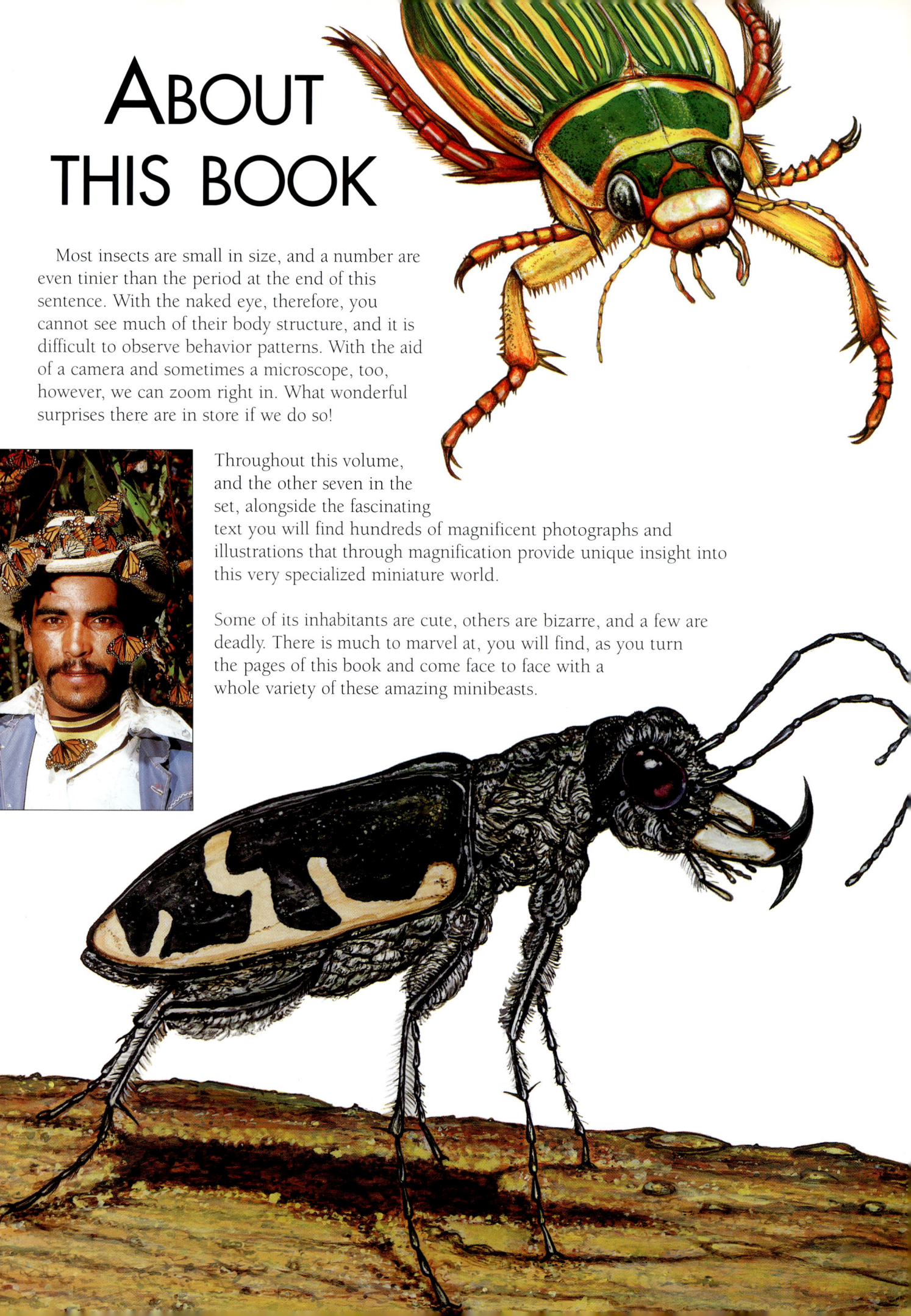

Most insects are small in size, and a number are even tinier than the period at the end of this sentence. With the naked eye, therefore, you cannot see much of their body structure, and it is difficult to observe behavior patterns. With the aid of a camera and sometimes a microscope, too, however, we can zoom right in. What wonderful surprises there are in store if we do so!

Throughout this volume, and the other seven in the set, alongside the fascinating text you will find hundreds of magnificent photographs and illustrations that through magnification provide unique insight into this very specialized miniature world.

Some of its inhabitants are cute, others are bizarre, and a few are deadly. There is much to marvel at, you will find, as you turn the pages of this book and come face to face with a whole variety of these amazing minibeasts.

# CONTENTS

| | |
|---|---|
| Introduction | 6 |
| Liftoff! | 8 |
| On the wing | 10 |
| Acrobatics | 12 |
| Great swimmers | 14 |
| Confident climbers | 16 |
| Off to sunnier climates | 18 |
| On the hop | 20 |
| On the march | 22 |
| Going underground | 24 |
| Slow movers | 26 |
| Skimming along | 28 |
| Minilegs | 30 |
| Easy riders | 32 |
| A speedy species | 34 |
| Moving in for the kill | 36 |
| Let's dance! | 38 |
| Hanging around | 40 |
| Immigrants | 42 |
| Making tracks | 44 |
| Glossary | 46 |
| Set index | 47 |

# INTRODUCTION

**Winter migration**
When the chilly days of fall arrive, instead of hibernating, millions of butterflies set off to sunnier regions such as Florida or Mexico, as described on pages 18-19.

Being able to get around is vital for most living creatures. They need to feed, find a mate, colonize new areas, perhaps, and escape from predators. However, no group of animals has found as many different ways of achieving such aims as the insects. Whether they jump, wriggle, walk, fly, hop, skate, or use jet propulsion, most insects will have perfected some form of motion and will always use it to their advantage. However, a number are extremely crafty and do not bother to expend any energy at all when getting from place to place. They simply hitch a ride. Others will hardly move at all once they are mature.

**On the march**
Some insects march for most of the time in long columns and form killer armies. You can meet them on pages 22-23.

But how do flying insects launch themselves into the air? Is it true that some march in huge armies? And why do a few migrate long distances? You are bound to be amazed by the very versatile movers of the insect kingdom.

**On the hop**
Which insects excel at hopping? Fleas can jump to great heights, but there are other insects, too, that leap, as you will discover if you take a look at pages 20-21.

**Speedy species**
Discover how some insects move with extraordinary speed by turning to pages 34-35. Some, you will find, can run or swim far faster than you!

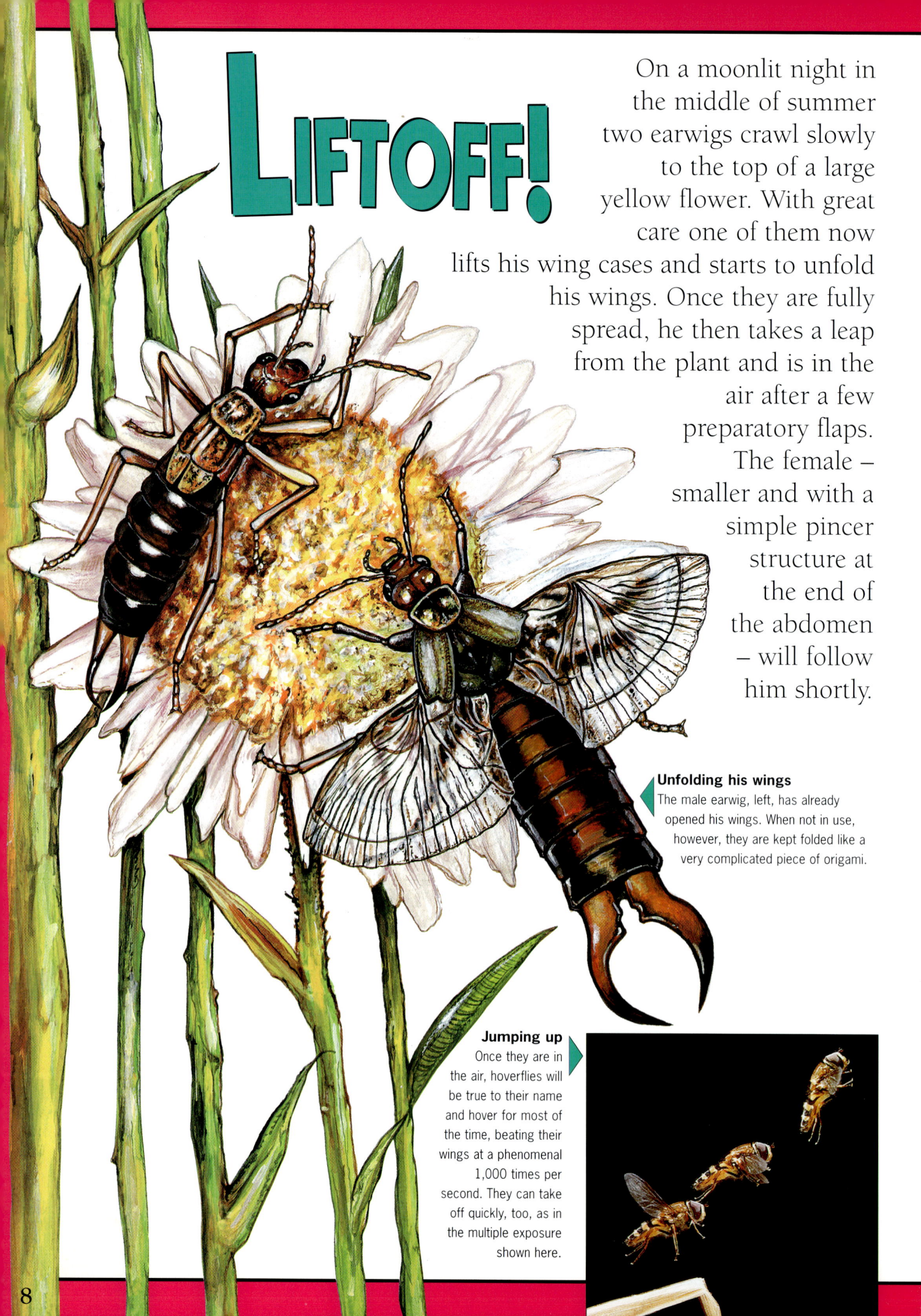

# LIFTOFF!

On a moonlit night in the middle of summer two earwigs crawl slowly to the top of a large yellow flower. With great care one of them now lifts his wing cases and starts to unfold his wings. Once they are fully spread, he then takes a leap from the plant and is in the air after a few preparatory flaps. The female – smaller and with a simple pincer structure at the end of the abdomen – will follow him shortly.

◀ **Unfolding his wings**
The male earwig, left, has already opened his wings. When not in use, however, they are kept folded like a very complicated piece of origami.

**Jumping up** ▶
Once they are in the air, hoverflies will be true to their name and hover for most of the time, beating their wings at a phenomenal 1,000 times per second. They can take off quickly, too, as in the multiple exposure shown here.

▲ **Away we go!**
In this multiflash image taken at night, you can see three stages of takeoff as an iron prominent moth from Europe launches itself from a leaf.

**A flying leap** ▶
This ichneumon fly – not a true fly but in the same order as wasps – has just taken off from a dead branch. Its flight looks particularly graceful because of its long body. It is parasitic and probably looking for a host on which to lay its eggs.

All species of earwigs with large, delicate hindwings always keep them folded under their *tegmina*, or wing cases, when at rest. The process of folding and unfolding them is extremely complicated. There may even be as many as 40 layers of wing. (If you take a piece of paper that is the same size as this page and try to fold it 40 times, you will see how difficult it is to do this. An earwig's wings are minute in comparison and so much harder to fold.)

## ACHIEVING FLIGHT

We know from fossil evidence that winged insects have existed for over 300 million years. Possibly, paleontologists have suggested, wings first developed among aquatic insects that had paddles for getting around in and on the water. These "paddles" may have become larger and more powerful with time, so that speed increased dramatically. These organs then became more like wings, and liftoff was a further natural development.

Only adult insects have fully developed and functional wings, although they can sometimes be seen as wing buds in an insect nymph. To achieve liftoff, an insect has to overcome both gravity and resistance to movement. It will use its legs to spring into the air and then activates its flight muscles.

◀ **Overcoming gravity**
When a cardinal beetle takes to the air, it first takes a little hop. At the same time, its nervous system makes the bright wing cases open. It is soon overcoming gravity.

▲ **Open cases**
The front wings of beetles have evolved into hard cases known as elytra. They protect the more delicate hindwings when the insect is not using them. The elytra still have a function, however, providing lift as they open so that the beetle can take to the air.

# ON THE WING

▲ **Fast transport**
This leaf-cutting bee is so strong that she can fly with a section of some birch foliage to her burrow.

Hovering in midair, a dragonfly uses its large eyes to scan for its prey. With luck a mosquito will emerge from the waterside reeds. The dragonfly will then alter the pitch of its wings and swoop toward it. Sometimes such a chase is dramatic; but the mosquito's flying skills are inferior, and the dragonfly will usually succeed in snapping up a snack.

Dragonflies beat their wings at around 20 up-and-down movements per second. They can also operate each of their four wings independently, which helps with taking off, flying backward, and hovering. Such powerful flight mechanisms also help insects find mates either singly or in a swarm; and those that are strong fliers but cannot survive in very cold temperatures – some butterflies, for instance – may be able to use their wings to migrate to warmer climates until spring returns.

◄ **High-speed action**
The camera has frozen a moment in time as an elephant hawk moth is in full flight. Its magnificent pink and olive wings have a span of over two inches. It is found mainly in Europe, as well as parts of Asia.

**Swift sand wasp**
Wasps rely on indirect flight muscles when taking to the air. They raise and lower the walls of the thorax so that the wings move up and down.

**On the beat**
Dragonflies have superb control over their wings. They can even take off in reverse and come to a standstill in midair. Then they hover on the spot while they beat their wings at an incredibly fast rate.

Flight muscles play a very important part in propelling an insect along. There are two types of muscles involved – direct and indirect. Dragonflies, mantises, grasshoppers, and beetles rely mostly on their *direct* flight muscles that are attached to their wings. Inner muscles pull down the base of each wing so that it goes up. Outer muscles then contract and pull the wings down.

Flies, bees, wasps, and butterflies, however, are more reliant on *indirect* flight muscles. They are attached to the walls of the thorax, not to the wings.

11

**Topsy-turvy**
Flies are not only so speedy that they are almost impossible to catch, they can even land the wrong way up so that their feet seem to dangle from the roof. It is a landing position that does not bother them at all.

# ACROBATICS

Have you ever watched flies do a half-spin, land, and then walk upside down on the ceiling, just as the fantasy character Spiderman might do? Flies can perform in this way without slipping or stumbling at all and may remain the wrong way up for quite some time before taking to the air again. They can climb up and down walls, too, without any difficulty. Thanks to the sticky pads on the soles of their feet, they have a firm grip on both horizontal and vertical surfaces. What superb acrobats flies are!

Hovering on the spot and moving backward in the air can also be counted among a fly's talents. Its *halteres*, or modified hindwings, are used to stabilize the insect in flight. They are particularly helpful when it comes to performing what to us seem to be amazing tricks. Dragonflies can also go backward and may turn somersaults in the air at times. In fact, it is their flying speed and agility that help them both catch a meal and escape many predators that might otherwise only too easily make a meal of them.

## TWIST AND SHOUT
Other insects are superb acrobats, too, and in several cases their antics are again vital to survival. If they happen to fall upside down on their backs, click beetles, for example, can throw themselves up to one foot in the air and straighten their stance so that they land the right way up once more, to the accompaniment of a loud clicking sound. Mating, meanwhile, may require considerable acrobatic activity for a number of insects and in a few species may even take place on the wing.

**Taking the plunge**
This mantis nymph is not yet mature; but even at this early stage falling from one surface to another does not present any difficulties. Its wings have not yet formed, otherwise it might have used them to ensure a safe landing.

### Almost a headstand
This katydid may appear to be performing a sort of headstand on a leaf, but it is putting on a warning display. The purpose is to frighten off a predator by looking far stronger and more athletic than it actually is.

### Like a limbo dancer
Hanging on for dear life with its six true legs and additional tiny stumps, known as prolegs or false legs, this moth caterpillar appears to be bending backward around a curved stem, in a posture like that of a limbo dancer. Its body is very flexible, or it would not be able to do this.

### Balancing act
It may look as if the pair of damselflies in this photograph are performing a sort of circus tightrope act, but they are in fact in their mating position. The male is on the stem, and both will contort their bodies so that his sperm can enter the female. They may even fly around like this for a while, as if harnessed together.

**▲ Lively larvae**
Seen dangling from pondweed, this dragonfly larva spends around four years underwater before reaching adulthood. It excels as an aquatic predator.

**In the water**
Midges (tiny flies) do not enter the water as adults, but their larvae, shown below, creep into fast streams. They have gills to help them breathe underwater. At the end of the pupal stage they float to the surface and break out of the pupae to fly away.

# Great Swimmers

Hanging motionless just below the water's surface, a predatory diving beetle waits patiently. As soon as it spies a smaller insect that it fancies for its lunch, however, two oarlike back legs spring out from the sides of its smooth, shiny body, and with a couple of thrusts the beetle starts to hurtle through the water at a tremendous rate. It will soon catch its prey.

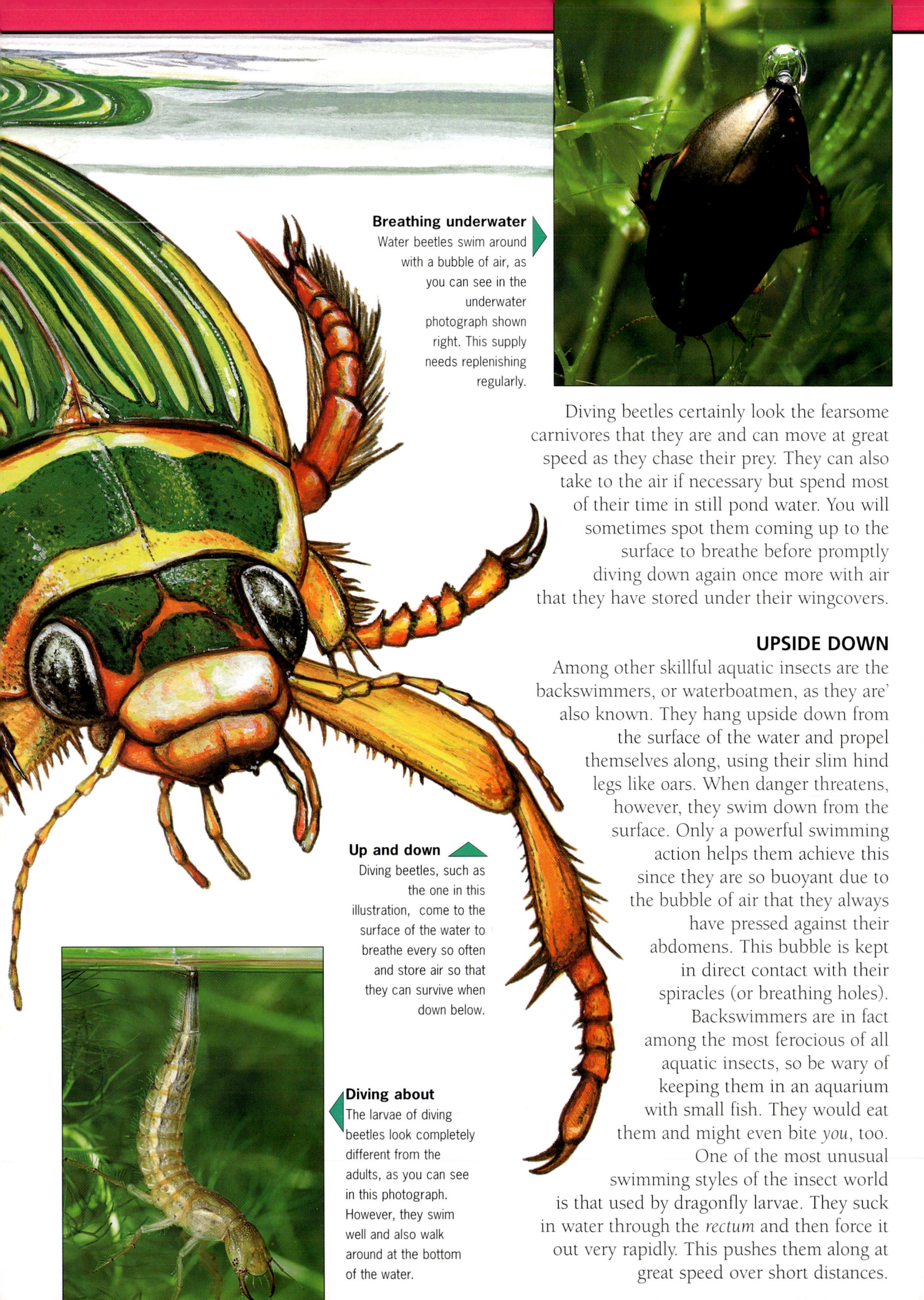

**Breathing underwater**
Water beetles swim around with a bubble of air, as you can see in the underwater photograph shown right. This supply needs replenishing regularly.

Diving beetles certainly look the fearsome carnivores that they are and can move at great speed as they chase their prey. They can also take to the air if necessary but spend most of their time in still pond water. You will sometimes spot them coming up to the surface to breathe before promptly diving down again once more with air that they have stored under their wingcovers.

## UPSIDE DOWN

Among other skillful aquatic insects are the backswimmers, or waterboatmen, as they are' also known. They hang upside down from the surface of the water and propel themselves along, using their slim hind legs like oars. When danger threatens, however, they swim down from the surface. Only a powerful swimming action helps them achieve this since they are so buoyant due to the bubble of air that they always have pressed against their abdomens. This bubble is kept in direct contact with their spiracles (or breathing holes).

Backswimmers are in fact among the most ferocious of all aquatic insects, so be wary of keeping them in an aquarium with small fish. They would eat them and might even bite *you*, too.

One of the most unusual swimming styles of the insect world is that used by dragonfly larvae. They suck in water through the *rectum* and then force it out very rapidly. This pushes them along at great speed over short distances.

**Up and down**
Diving beetles, such as the one in this illustration, come to the surface of the water to breathe every so often and store air so that they can survive when down below.

**Diving about**
The larvae of diving beetles look completely different from the adults, as you can see in this photograph. However, they swim well and also walk around at the bottom of the water.

15

# CONFIDENT CLIMBERS

A shiny tortoise beetle has found a fresh, juicy leaf on which to chew and is enjoying its supper. However, the tree on which she is feeding is protected by a vicious army that does not welcome her presence. They regard the plant as theirs, particularly since there are aphids around that they cannot resist milking for delicious honeydew. Seconds after the beetle's jaws have sunk into the tasty foliage, a horde of ants suddenly comes along the branch and spills over onto that very leaf. Instantly, the beetle grips the leaf as hard as she can, pulling her body down flush with its surface. She is determined to remain there. However hard the ants try, they will not be able to dislodge her and will eventually give up. The tortoise beetle has succeeded in staking a claim to that part of the plant.

▲ **A firm grip**
Ants can scuttle up and down vegetation without too much trouble, but they are not nearly as tenacious as some beetles in holding onto the surface along which they are crawling. The grip of tortoise beetles, for example, is very strong, and it can be hard to get them to budge from where they have a foothold.

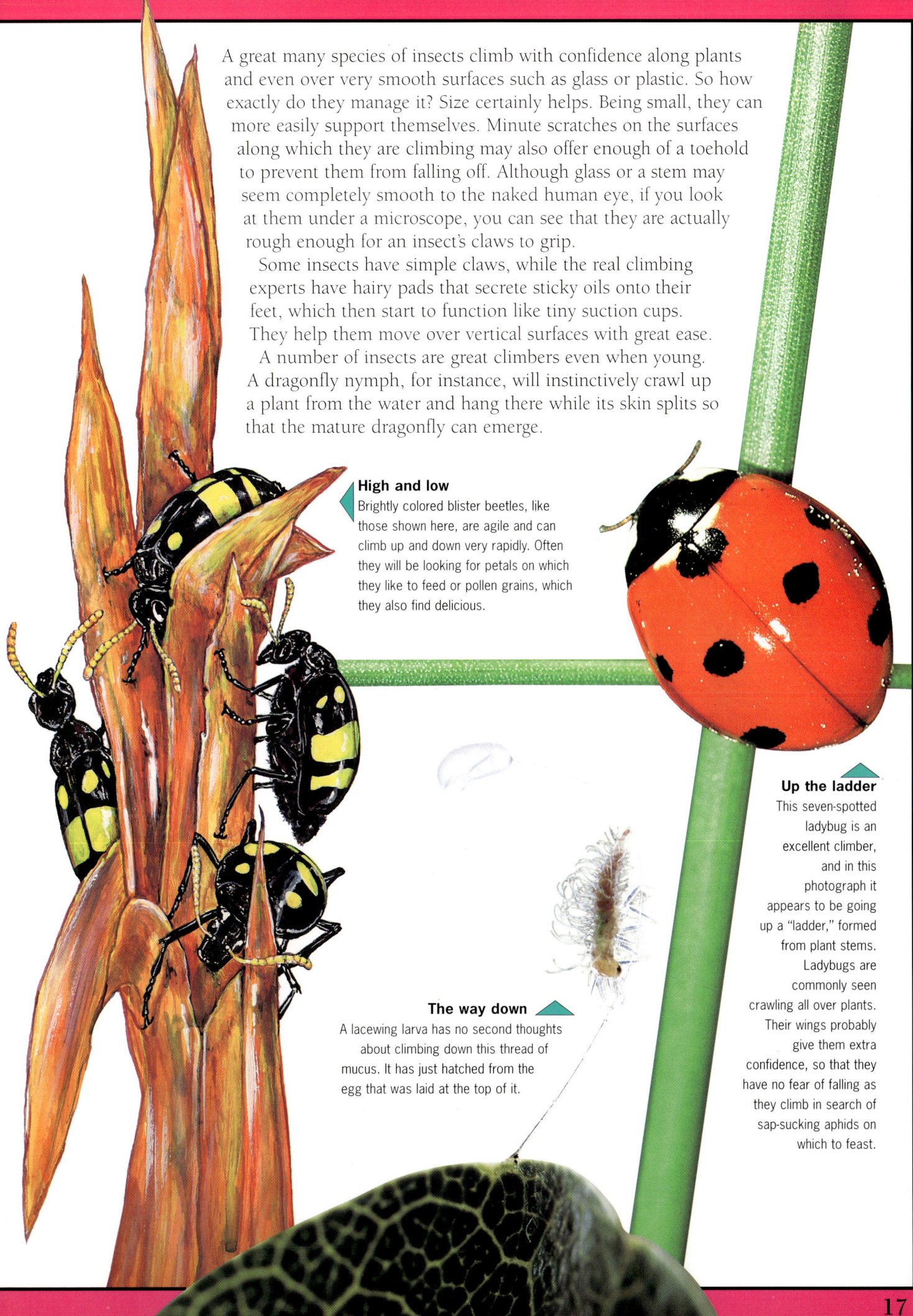

A great many species of insects climb with confidence along plants and even over very smooth surfaces such as glass or plastic. So how exactly do they manage it? Size certainly helps. Being small, they can more easily support themselves. Minute scratches on the surfaces along which they are climbing may also offer enough of a toehold to prevent them from falling off. Although glass or a stem may seem completely smooth to the naked human eye, if you look at them under a microscope, you can see that they are actually rough enough for an insect's claws to grip.

Some insects have simple claws, while the real climbing experts have hairy pads that secrete sticky oils onto their feet, which then start to function like tiny suction cups. They help them move over vertical surfaces with great ease.

A number of insects are great climbers even when young. A dragonfly nymph, for instance, will instinctively crawl up a plant from the water and hang there while its skin splits so that the mature dragonfly can emerge.

**High and low**
Brightly colored blister beetles, like those shown here, are agile and can climb up and down very rapidly. Often they will be looking for petals on which they like to feed or pollen grains, which they also find delicious.

**Up the ladder**
This seven-spotted ladybug is an excellent climber, and in this photograph it appears to be going up a "ladder," formed from plant stems. Ladybugs are commonly seen crawling all over plants. Their wings probably give them extra confidence, so that they have no fear of falling as they climb in search of sap-sucking aphids on which to feast.

**The way down**
A lacewing larva has no second thoughts about climbing down this thread of mucus. It has just hatched from the egg that was laid at the top of it.

17

▲ **Migrants**
Once each year, in certain parts of North America you can see millions of monarch butterflies wending their way to Mexico or Florida, where it will be warmer.

# Off to Sunnier Climates

In parts of Canada, as the days start to get shorter, a cloud starts to form on the horizon to the north. Slowly, it gets bigger and is soon overhead. This cloud is not made of water vapor, however. As it passes, those people below it can just about pick out the orange and black wings of thousands of butterflies as they travel at about 20 miles per hour and at a height of 75 feet above ground level. The huge swarm is flying south to warmer weather. The 2,000-mile journey will be a hard one for these delicate creatures with a wingspan of only three to four inches. They are off to Florida, California, or Mexico. On the way they will rest by night on trees, moving on again at daybreak. Once they arrive at their destination, they will be able to avoid the shiveringly low temperatures of a typical Canadian winter.

▲ **Birth places**
Monarch butterfly females lay in North America in spring or summer, or in Mexico or Florida, where they spend the winter. From their eggs emerge brightly patterned caterpillars, like the one in the photograph above.

**Mexican holiday**
The Mexican in the photograph, right, stands still and tries not to disturb the visiting North American monarch butterflies that are using his head and his body as a landing strip. They have flown south to overwinter in a warmer region.

Curiously, when the time comes for monarch butterflies to return to Canada, they do not fly in such huge swarms but more as individuals or in small groups, so that it is difficult to plot their movement. What is most remarkable, however, is that monarchs arrive at the same trees in southern regions year after year, even though none of them ever lives to make the journey twice. The sites that they occupy are protected by law in Mexico, but as a result of illegal logging some of this temporary winter haven has unfortunately been destroyed over recent years.

## LONG-HAUL FLIGHTS

Monarchs have been introduced to Australia, and a similar pattern of migration has been discovered, although time and direction are reversed because this continent is south of the equator. They are not the only butterflies to migrate. Red admirals, for example, fly to Great Britain from the Mediterranean in the spring and some may return southward before winter. Painted ladies and clouded yellows also migrate. In 1960 an interesting experiment took place that proved the huge distances that even very small moths may fly when they migrate. Nuclear tests had taken place in the Sahara Desert during February. Later that year an entomologist working in the United Kingdom tested some moths he had caught and that were known to have migrated from Africa. On them he found traces of radioactivity that definitely was linked to the North African tests.

**An emerging monarch**
The monarch butterfly, right, has just emerged from the pupal case in which it spent its resting stage before taking on its adult form. When the weather is warmer in North America, it will return from Mexico to the region of the Great Lakes.

### ▲ Froghoppers
These small insects are up to half an inch long and are named because of their froglike leaping on the plants and shrubs on which they feed. They closely resemble leafhoppers but have fewer spines on their hindlegs.

### Leaping locusts
Locusts are a large type of grasshopper, and they can hop and fly, as you can see in the photograph shown right. When their back legs are extended, they reach way past the abdomen and help them take huge, bounding leaps.

### ▲ Leafhoppers
As they hop from plant to plant, leafhoppers frequently spread plant diseases and are also serious crop pests. They are common jumping insects and look much like froghoppers, except that they have slimmer bodies.

# On the Hop

As the weak spring sunlight warms the bark of a fallen tree, a chipmunk jumps down, and his movement disturbs the blanket covering of thousands of springtails. They leap away in panic; and even though they are tiny, the combined effect is bewildering to the chipmunk, who runs for cover. The force with which the springtails launch themselves takes them several times their own body length into the air.

### ◀ Springing about
Even though it is under one-quarter of an inch long, a springtail still has remarkable control over its body movement. It has a special leaping organ known as a furcula at its rear. It is held underneath by a catch but released when the insect wants to hop, so that it is tossed into the air.

### ▲ Into the air
In this photograph, while one grasshopper looks on, another leaps toward a different stem. Grasshoppers have strongly muscled back legs that are used for leaping. Most also have wings but rarely use them for short trips.

### Treehoppers ▲
Jumping is also something at which treehoppers excel. They can be recognized by the projection that extends back over the thorax. They suck at sap and hop on the surface of leaves, often in large groups.

Whether they hop to escape predators or simply as an efficient means of moving, lots of insects are past masters at springing around. Several different techniques are used to help them hop. Some have strong back legs with special fibers that act like rubber bands, for example. Not all use their legs, however. Some call on other body parts, such as the tips of their abdomens, to help them into the air.

Springtails have developed a very unusual way of getting around. The last two segments of their body have evolved into a long spike. While the insect is just walking, it is held under the body with its tip slotted into a notch on the underside of the abdomen. If danger threatens, however, the spike is released, and the insect is flung several inches into the air. This is, of course, how the springtail gets its name.

### Prize jumper ▶
Just as energy powers the spring of a pogo stick when you play with one, stored energy powers a flea's mighty leaps.

## GREAT HEIGHTS
Perhaps the greatest hopper of all, however, is the flea. With its enlarged hind legs and streamlined body, it can leap with tremendous force as it makes use of a special hard pad in the thorax that is made from a remarkable elastic substance known as *resilin*. Through the use of high-speed photography a lot has been learned about the way fleas achieve the heights to which they jump. As they gather their legs, the elastic pad is bent. Sudden release then provides stored energy for the leap. No artificial material has ever been manufactured with as much elasticity as resilin. If engineers could do this, they would probably be able to produce balls that would bounce as high as a two-story house, or even higher, without any problem at all.

▲ **Strong and speedy**
This harvester ant has just found a thistle seed and will march with it back to its underground nest. Others will accompany it, going along in single file.

# On the March

With slashing jaws a fast-moving colony of stinging army ants is on the march on the floor of a South American forest. Any unlucky insects, such as moths, that fail to get out of the column's way are soon overpowered. Their bodies will be cut up for food, and the ants will then carry on marching. Many larger animals, too, would rather get out of the ants' path than face the agony of such an attack. Army ants not only move quickly, they like their own way and will fight to the death to achieve it.

Even though many insect species cannot fly, a number still manage to move huge distances in search of food. Indeed, some may gather in vast armies, devouring almost everything in their path. With so many mouths to feed it is important to keep moving, or many might starve to death.

Army ants, only about half an inch long, can move at 10 feet per minute, which is 11 miles per hour. If you think this is slow, bear in mind that a small car is about 450 times the length of an ant. Multiply the ant's speed by 450, and you will see that its speed is actually the equivalent of around 50 mph – a great deal faster than you or any other human being can run!

It is a killer army, and these ants will even feed on creatures several times their own size. Soldier ants stay on the outside of the army ant column and defend it. The queen, meanwhile, marches in the center with the workers who carry her eggs and the larvae. There is no single leader to the huge column, but ants are social insects and take turns at heading the march. It is rare for the unit to stop; but when the larvae are about to pupate before full adulthood, it will rest for a while and then again start the long march to no definite destination.

**At the double**
Soldier army ants, like the one shown above, are quick on their long legs and will stay on the outside of a marching column to guard it from any predators that dare to approach the moving colony as it goes along at the double.

**Dangerous journey**
These termites, photographed in the rainforest of Malaysia, are looking for leaves that they will bring back to their fungus garden. Their great enemies are the army ants, so they will be lucky not to meet some.

**Advance of the army**
Army ant columns are sometimes as much as ten feet wide. Most of the day is spent marching but they rest by night. Scouts sometimes break away from a column to forage for food.

▲ **Excavating a nest**
The bumblebee queen, shown in the photograph above, is busy digging a nest that will contain several branching tunnels. They will be lined with mud. Within them, brood cells will be constructed, and one egg will be laid in each.

▲ **It's the pits!**
These pits in the ground are a sure sign that there are antlions below the surface. They wait there to pounce on any prey that comes along.

◀ **Whose hole?**
This mysterious hole leads to an ant nest underground. In some species of ant, it is the queen who starts the nest; in others, it is the workers.

# GOING

In a tiny underground cell, hardly more than an inch long, a mud wasp has laid an egg. The emerging grub will not go hungry even though its mother has abandoned it. Sharing its miniature home are several jumping spiders that the mother wasp caught for it.

# UNDERGROUND

She did this before she had even finished the nest and prior to laying. The spiders were stung and paralyzed by her and therefore could not escape. In time they will be eaten by the grub. It has a strong appetite, but the nest is more than adequately stocked.

An underground home is one of the safest places for an insect, and many spend at least part of their lives hidden below the surface. Some have evolved powerful digging legs, and others have jaws that act like shovels so that they can scoop their way down into the soil without too much difficulty.

Cockchafers, also known as maybugs, burrow into the earth to a depth of about five inches both by boring with their pointed abdomens and scraping with their forefeet, and here they will deposit up to 40 eggs. The grubs feed on plant roots for about four years and become so plump that they can hardly move. But they soon have to go deeper into the earth in order to hollow out a cell in which they will pupate well away from predators. There is more movement beneath your feet than you might ever have imagined.

**Champion digger**
Photographed in Austria, this mole cricket spends most of its time burrowing and has front legs that are ideally shaped for digging.

**Down below**
In a tiny underground nest, a group of jumping spiders is paralyzed and stands rooted to the spot. When the wasp larva hatches from the egg that you can see, there will be more than enough for it to feed on until it matures. The mother mud wasp is a good provider.

# SLOW MOVERS

**Motionless moth**
The female vaporer moth has no wings and in fact hardly looks like a moth at all. She will lay lots of eggs after mating but is lifeless in comparison with the male. He flies well and is much more mothlike in appearance and behavior.

Having wriggled free from her tight pupal case, a female vaporer moth has at last emerged into the light. She is one of an unusual species. Unlike most moths, she will never develop fully formed wings and fly. Instead, her tightly crumpled wings remain that way. Dragging her bloated body slowly along a twig, she stops after having moved only a few inches. Then, as if exhausted, she will rest, her abdomen swaying slightly in the breeze. Staying here, she waits patiently for a male to come along and mate with her. With her last reserves of energy she will lay her eggs.

**Camouflaged chrysalis**
Unlike the female vaporer moth, the elephant hawk moth shown in this photograph will fly energetically once it is mature. During its resting stage in a chrysalis, however, it remains virtually immobile and will usually be superbly camouflaged.

### Legless larva
At home in a dead holly stump, this stag beetle larva has no real legs as yet and so can only wriggle along very slowly, feeding on the wood as it tunnels its way through.

### Just like fixtures
Photographed on a bay tree, female scale insects hardly move at all and remain attached to their host plant. The males, however, which are not often seen, are a little more active.

Some insects hardly seem to move at all. Stick insects, for example, will usually remain immobile by day, restricting any movement to after dark, when they are less likely to be spotted and so can feed without risk of attack. Even if they are accidentally knocked off a branch, by the wind perhaps, they simply fall to the ground and lie still, refusing to draw attention to themselves.

## CRAWLING ALONG
The larvae of some beetles are also slow movers. They have no legs at all and so can only wriggle along as they chew tunnels through the wood in which they live. Fly maggots have no legs either. Like wood beetles, they have no need to move quickly. The eggs will normally have been laid on a food supply such as rotting meat or dung, so that they do not have to hunt for a source of nourishment. Such lack of movement at this early stage in their lives makes it all the more surprising that they will eventually become speedy fliers.

Caterpillars, too, can be slow movers, working their way along by releasing one pair of legs at a time and then pushing themselves forward with a wavelike movement. The chrysalises that they become before the adult moth or butterfly stage, however, are generally completely immobile. Some chrysalises, however, move if a predator threatens them.

Slow-moving insects will often have difficulty in escaping from predators. Some manage to find a way around this. Scale insects, for instance, will secrete a waxy substance. This coats their backs and makes them look very unappetizing.

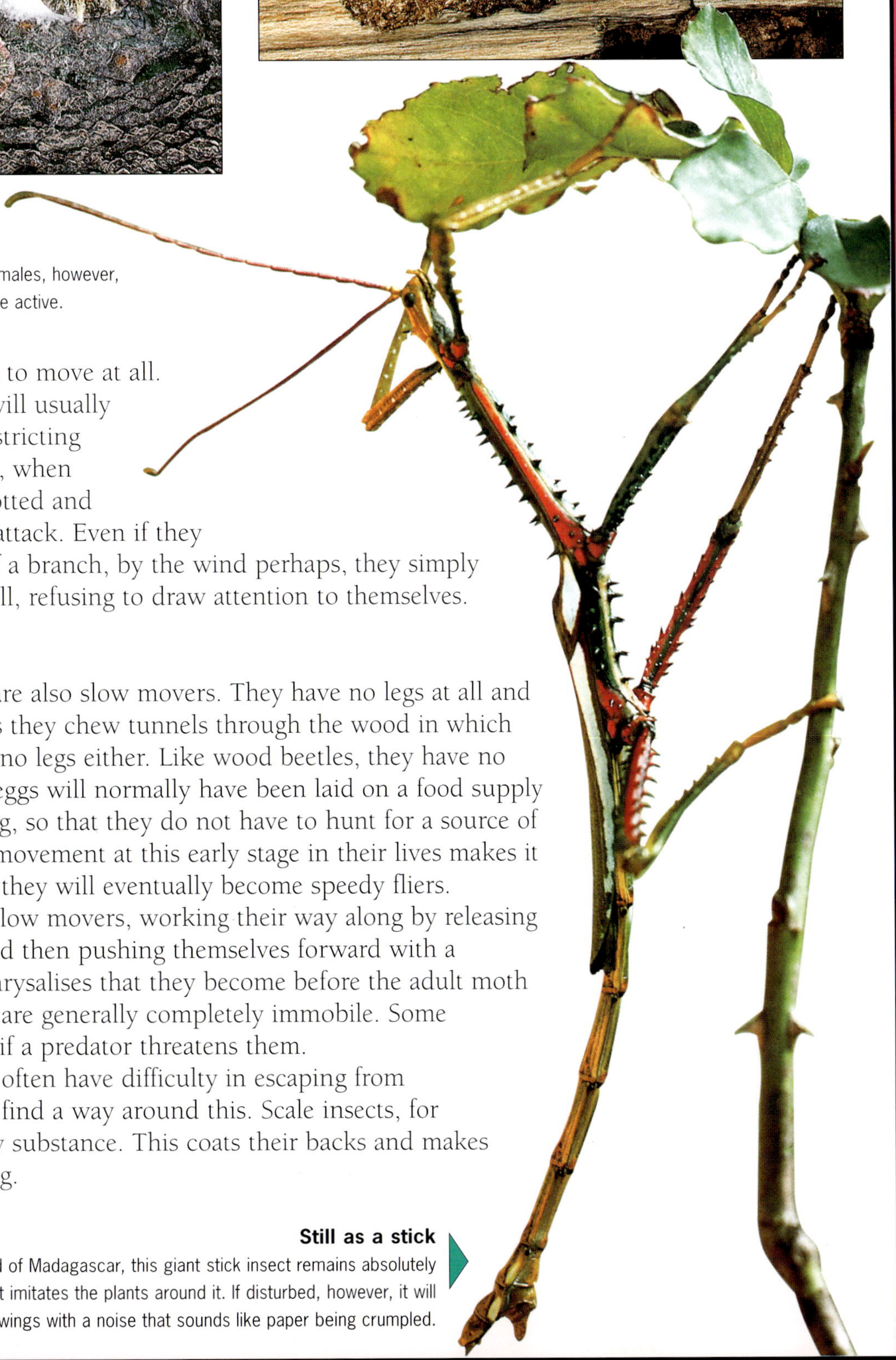

### Still as a stick
Native to the island of Madagascar, this giant stick insect remains absolutely stationary by day as it imitates the plants around it. If disturbed, however, it will suddenly open its wings with a noise that sounds like paper being crumpled.

# Skimming Along

**Walking on water**
The bodies of pond-skaters are covered with silver water-repellent hairs that prevent them from becoming too damp. They frequently jump considerable distances but never break the water's surface. Their hind legs steer them along.

**Fast and furious**
Pond-skaters are so quick on their feet as they skim the surface of the water that these carnivores can easily catch an unwary insect such as the bee in this photograph. It had only come to the pond for a drink but lost its life to the skater.

Two very long-legged pond-skaters appear to be resting on the still surface of a pond but are always at the ready. Suitable prey might chance to wander by, and if so, the two predators will pounce. If one type of rove beetle is in the vicinity, however, they may not be so lucky, and a deadly skating competition, with the loser ending up as lunch, might begin. This rove beetle has a remarkable method of moving. It can secrete a drop of fluid from the tip of its abdomen, and the fluid will lower the surface tension of the water behind it so that it is drawn forward at a rapid rate without much effort. This is a fantastic means of making a speedy get-away to safety or of accelerating in the role of predator.

### Darting around
This skimmer dragonfly, resting on a fragrant waterlily, is an excellent flier. As its name suggests, it particularly excels at skimming over water.

### Treading the surface
Pond-skaters are so confident and stable on the surface of the water that they can even mate there, as shown in this photograph.

Insects weigh so little that they can frequently take advantage of the phenomenon of surface tension. Indeed, if they are light enough and can spread their weight, they are able, literally, to walk on water without going through the surface. Then, by using rowing motions with their legs, they can skate around on the surface at an impressive rate. If they are predatory, the surface of the water will also help them track down their prey. Any movement on the surface will make ripples travel outward. Then all the predatory insects have to do is home in on their prey. Backswimmers, meanwhile, skate upside down just below the surface of the water. This stance seems to be controlled by light. In fact, scientists have found that if these small but fierce carnivorous insects are placed in a tank lighted from below, they start to swim the right way up, not on their backs.

## OVER THE OCEAN
Sea-skaters, meanwhile, though possibly hundreds of miles from the nearest land mass, move in the same way as pond-skaters but over the deep ocean surfaces. Some dragonflies will also skim along over ponds, pools, lakes, streams, or rivers before mating. The females will lay their eggs on reeds, in mud, or in the actual water.

# Minilegs

**A matter of balance**
Caterpillars sometimes have to wriggle along awkward surfaces as they go in search of more food to satisfy their seemingly insatiable appetites, as shown here.

A hawkmoth caterpillar has worked its way to the top of a stalk and is holding onto it with its three pairs of short legs. Without these appendages it would not be able to walk, climb, or guide leaves into its jaws. But they are not its only legs. Further back along its body it has other stumpy muscular projections that support its weight and also act as aids to gripping.

**Creepy-crawlies**
These brightly colored larvae of the blue-barred morpho butterfly, photographed in Guyana, need not only their six "real" legs but also their prolegs, or "false" legs, to help them cling to the underside of a leaf.

**Clawed appendages**
Feeding on ragwort, this cinnabar moth caterpillar works its way along the plant with undulating movements and remains stable thanks to the claws at the end of its stumpy prolegs.

**True or false?**
Take a careful look at the photograph shown here, and see if you can identify which are the caterpillar's "real" legs and which are its additional prolegs.

A caterpillar's six minilegs are attached to its thorax, each thoracic segment carrying one pair. (In some leaf-mining caterpillars, however, these legs are even smaller or absent altogether.) The abdomen, meanwhile, sometimes carries what are called either false legs, or *prolegs*. They are soft and fleshy, and broader at the body end. They help the caterpillar crawl along and feature a series of hooks that assist with balance. The surface of a leaf can be very slippery, particularly after it has rained, and these larvae need all the help they can muster to ensure that they will remain in place. The silk threads they exude are also useful in case they fall.

A caterpillar's prolegs are conical in shape and have a circle of hairs at the tips that keeps the larva stable as it moves. Next time you see a caterpillar, notice how it moves and uses its legs and prolegs with great efficiency.

**Hanging on tightly**
This strange-looking moth caterpillar is using all of its three pairs of tiny legs to grip the top of a yellowing stalk on which it is feeding. Further down its body are five pairs of clawed prolegs that help keep it from falling. In fact, if you have ever tried to remove a caterpillar from a stem, you will know how firmly it can hold onto a surface.

# EASY RIDERS

**Hitchhikers**
Red mites cling tightly to the thorax of a cranefly. They are both external and internal parasites, and so their presence is not welcome to this insect as they bum a ride.

The microscope takes us into another world completely. Study an insect's body parts under the lens, and you will not only see them highly enlarged but perhaps also be fortunate enough to spot a parasite that has been taking advantage of its host. Hatchling oil beetles, for instance, will frequently hitch a ride when a bee stops at a flower to feed. While the bee is preoccupied, the larva crawls into its fur. The bee takes to the air and ferries the tiny hitchhiker to its nest. Parasitic wingless bee lice also hitch rides. What better way could there be for an insect to get around if it has no winged transport of its own!

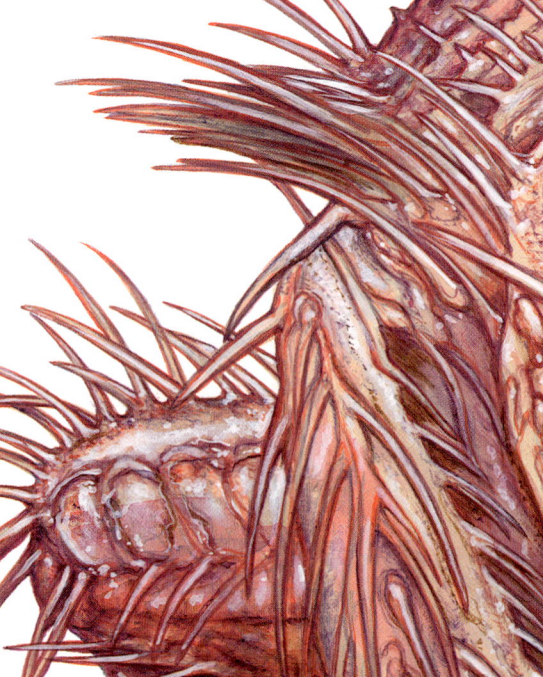

**Riding high**
Some tiny parasitic flies, also known as bee lice, have lost the use of their wings and rely on their claws for holding onto a bee's furry coat as the bee transports them from place to place. A bee louse has been magnified here at about 150 times life size.

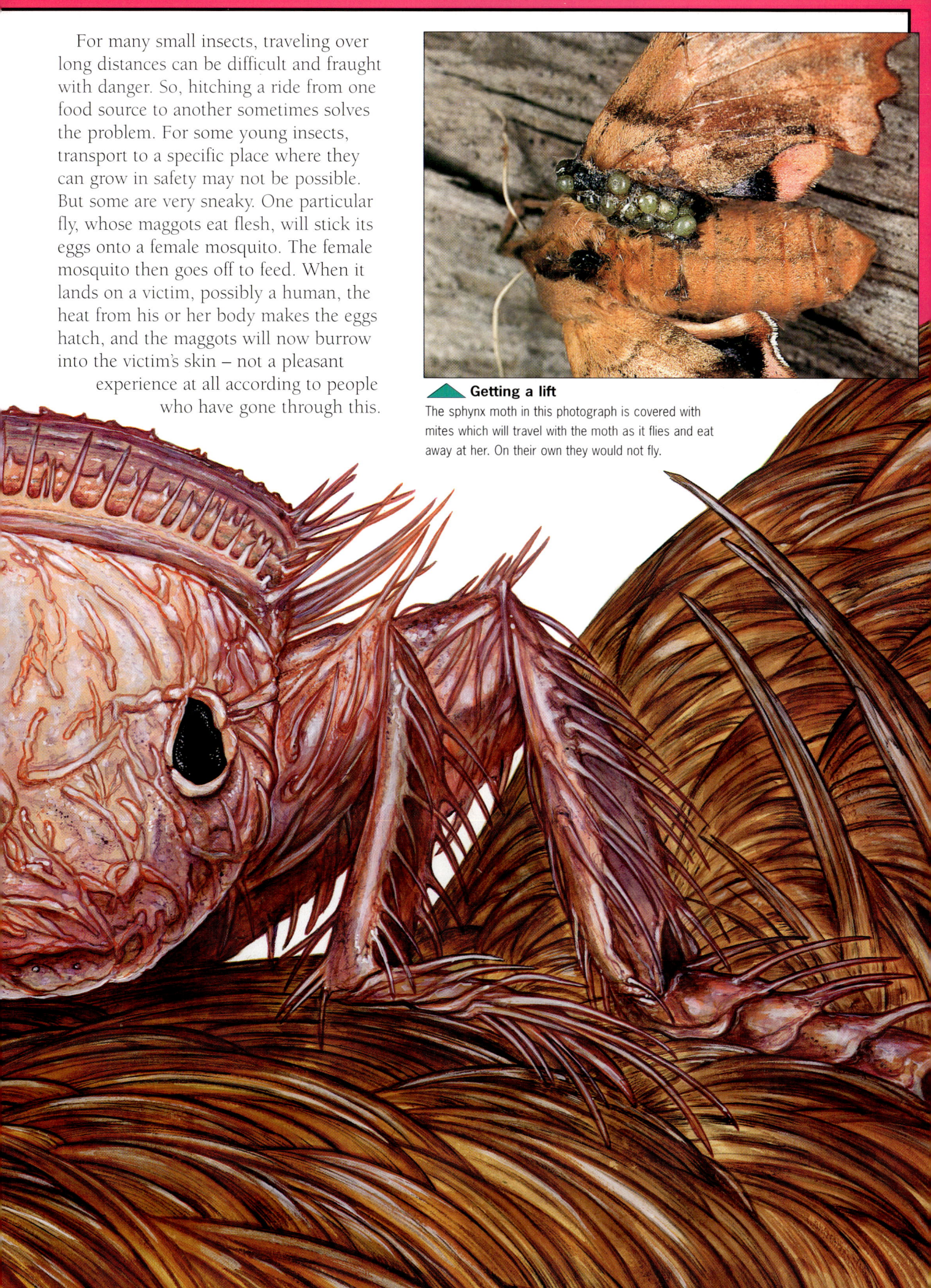

For many small insects, traveling over long distances can be difficult and fraught with danger. So, hitching a ride from one food source to another sometimes solves the problem. For some young insects, transport to a specific place where they can grow in safety may not be possible. But some are very sneaky. One particular fly, whose maggots eat flesh, will stick its eggs onto a female mosquito. The female mosquito then goes off to feed. When it lands on a victim, possibly a human, the heat from his or her body makes the eggs hatch, and the maggots will now burrow into the victim's skin – not a pleasant experience at all according to people who have gone through this.

### Getting a lift
The sphynx moth in this photograph is covered with mites which will travel with the moth as it flies and eat away at her. On their own they would not fly.

# A SPEEDY SPECIES

On a warm summer's morning a male long-legged tiger beetle is sunning itself on the ground before it gets too hot to be out in the open. He is constantly on the alert for a possible victim, however, as are the larvae of his species.

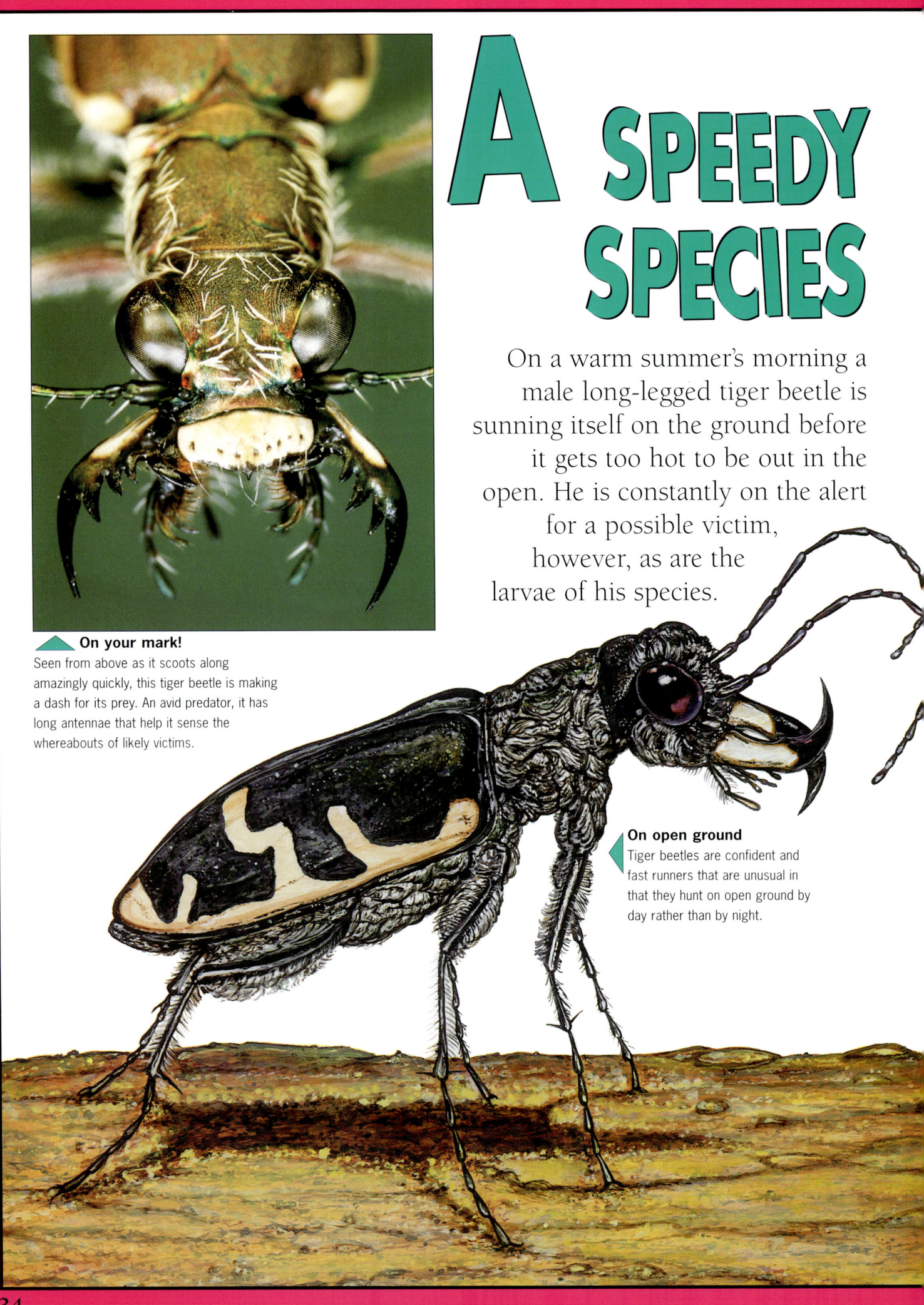

▲ **On your mark!**
Seen from above as it scoots along amazingly quickly, this tiger beetle is making a dash for its prey. An avid predator, it has long antennae that help it sense the whereabouts of likely victims.

◀ **On open ground**
Tiger beetles are confident and fast runners that are unusual in that they hunt on open ground by day rather than by night.

**Active by day**
A bright green tiger beetle has just overcome its prey in the photograph, left. This beetle loves the sun and only takes cover at night. The larvae, however, hunt from the entrance to their burrow.

A short while after hatching, tiger beetle larvae will be waiting at the entrance to their burrows, ever hungry for a meal. When the adult beetle spots a spider, quick as a flash he makes his approach. A very fast runner, he easily catches his quarry and rapidly devours it.

Most tiger beetles are heat-loving and can be found on dry soil or even on beaches. If the temperature gets too high for them, however, they will rapidly go underground. Some are so small that they would be virtually invisible were it not for their fast movement, which disturbs the soil or sand around them. When they take to the air, they dart about just as quickly as a fly does when disturbed, to the accompaniment of furious buzzing, too. Keen-eyed and with powerful mandibles, they make formidable predators.

**Capturing prey**
Its long legs stood the tiger beetle that is shown above in good stead. It caught up with its grasshopper prey and immediately began to tackle it.

In fact, catching up with them always requires more than a degree of persistence. Making allowances for the difference in size, they run at about the equivalent of twice the speed that *you* can achieve when sprinting, which is no mean feat.

**Racing ahead**
Among the fastest creatures on earth, tiger beetles can run like the wind. They are also ferocious, as their sickleshaped jaws and their name clearly indicate.

# Moving in for the Kill

**▲ Sucking at its prey**
Having lurked for a while in vegetation that provided good camouflage, the assassin bug in the photograph above suddenly pounced on a solitary bee and is now sucking it dry.

**▲ Mean mimic**
Some assassin bugs are mimics. The one in this photograph taken in Costa Rica, for example, mimics the tarantula wasp and is seen feeding on a scarab beetle.

**▲ Caterpillar catch**
This South African assassin bug has been successful in his hunt and is seen here eating his caterpillar prey.

Two assassin bugs, recognizable because of their curved beak or *rostrum*, leap out to attack an unsuspecting wasp. The aim is to grab at their prey and then to stab it with their sharp mouthparts. They will release toxic substances to paralyze their victim and then suck her dry before discarding her as an empty husk. However, just as the nearest assassin bug is about to snatch at the wasp, it swerves and manages to avoid the predator. Even insects as determined and skilled at hunting as assassin bugs do not always get their way.

Some assassin bugs can release a very effective venom. It has even been reported that the venom can be squirted with extreme force and aimed at an enemy *behind* the assassin bug if the insect twists its beak around. This can be repeated several times with astonishingly accurate marksmanship.

Humans, too, can suffer at the hands of some species of assassin bugs. The great naturalist Charles Darwin, for instance, recorded that some had crawled all over his body one night when he was in South America. Some time later Darwin developed an undiagnosed disease that proved incurable. It is now thought this was Chagas' disease, an illness known to be spread by assassin bugs and tsetse flies.

**◀ Nasty nymphs**
Assassin bug nymphs are also ferocious killers. The one in the photograph on the left is completely covered in sand, as well as its victims' corpses.

**Attack on two fronts**
Assassin bugs, like the two shown in this illustration, often pounce on pollinating insects, which they will try to paralyze by injecting an immobilizing chemical. If they succeed, the victim – in this case, a wasp – will not be able to fight back.

**Gyrating away**
If disturbed, entire colonies of this species of yellow aphids will start to dance, twisting their bodies in the attempt to stop predators.

# LET'S DANCE!

There is a lot of activity going on in the hive, and bees are busy exchanging information. A forager has recently returned to perform what is known as a round dance. The other bees appear fascinated by what she is doing. She has returned with some nectar and shares it while turning around in circles every few seconds as if the star act at a hive disco. Her dance is both energetic and noisy – sure signs that not only is the nectar of excellent quality, but that it is nearby. This is even more promising than yesterday, when another returned to perform a waggle dance, involving a figure-of-eight formation and much abdomen-shaking. That dance also provided information about a source of nectar, but the type of dance indicated the source to be further away.

When we dance, it is just a form of exercise or to show off. When bees start moving rhythmically, however, they have information to impart. Entomologists have proved this by marking a worker bee and giving it an artificial but rich food source. They then let it return to its home but prevented it from leaving the hive. Other workers from the same hive were nevertheless able to locate the food source, having obtained information as to its whereabouts from the imprisoned bee.

In another experiment almost all the workers who had made direct contact with a round-dancing messenger were able to find a new food source in under five minutes. Such *a round* dance indicates that flowers are fewer than 80 feet away, but a *waggle* dance performance announces that the food source may be as far as 300 feet from the hive.

The number of times the bee waggles its abdomen communicates the distance, and the angle at which the dance is performed signals the angle between the sun and the food supply. Scout bees also perform a special dance when they want to advise about a new nesting site. If there are several possible sites, they will dance at different angles for different lengths of time and at different speeds. It is as if they are discussing the suitability of each site. After more scouts have gone to assess the sites, they then indicate that a decision has been reached by performing the same dance routine. If, however, you see bees doing a sort of fan dance at the entrance to a hive, they are trying to cool it down.

**A fan dance**
It is midsummer, and these bees, photographed in New York State, are performing an energetic fan dance, flapping their wings in unison to ventilate their hive and to control the temperature inside.

**The round dance**
When a foraging bee comes back to its hive and spins around and around as it dances, as in this illustration, the others know that there is excellent nectar nearby.

**The waggle dance**
One of these honey bees has returned to the hive to perform the waggle dance, providing coded information about a distant food source.

39

# Hanging Around

**In midair**
A hummingbird hawk moth can beat its wings at up to 300 times each second. This movement is so fast that it is almost invisible as the moth remains suspended in the air.

Hummingbird hawk moths, like the one shown *above*, spend most of their time traveling from flower to flower or simply resting. Every now and then, however, as they fly, they will suddenly stop in midair and start to hover. If the flower over which they are hovering produces the sort of nectar that they like, without landing they will uncurl their long proboscis and start to suck up the sweet substance. They do this frequently since they need to boost their energy levels for all that speedy hovering.

**High-speed hover**
Hoverflies, as their name suggests, can hang in the air by beating their wings at an extremely fast rate, just like other superb hoverers. To achieve this, contact between the nervous system and their muscles must be very finely tuned.

**Just like a helicopter**
If you have ever watched a helicopter hovering over a site before landing, you will recognize a similar whirring of wings when a hoverbee approaches a flower.

Among the most amazing sights in the whole of the insect kingdom is the hovering of the hummingbird hawk moths. When they stop dead-still in the air, it is almost as if they must be hanging from some sort of invisible thread. Dragonflies can do this, too. Being able to hover has a number of advantages. Nectar-feeders will be able to approach flowers on which it might otherwise be difficult to land, and predatory insects will be able to maintain suitable vantage points from which to watch for prey. With their keen eyesight, powerful jaws, and grasping legs, dragonflies are well adapted for hunting; and when they hover in midair, they will be able to dart after a victim at the very first sign of one.

Some insects have incorporated hovering into their courtship rituals. Only a very healthy insect can generate enough energy to hover. Healthy genes will then be passed on so that the next generation is likely to be healthy, too.

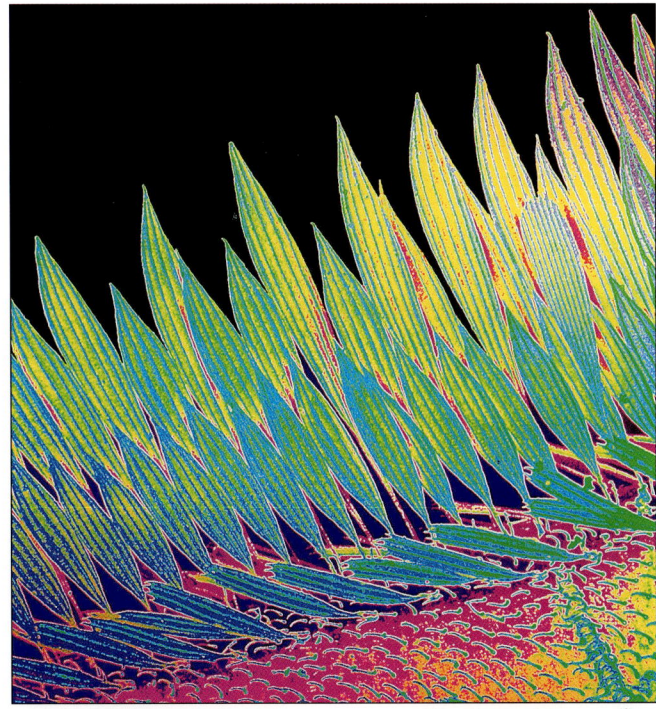

**Beating wings**
Among the most accomplished hoverers of all, mosquitoes beat their wings at a phenomenal rate. As they hover, the edges of their wings, shown above, pick up lots of information about environmental conditions.

**Flower power**
The nectar on which this soft-bodied, furry, beelike fly feeds provides the energy for it to hover over other flowers. Then, in turn, it will suck up more sweetness.

41

# IMMIGRANTS

**Biological control**
The larvae in the photograph above bore holes into prickly pear cacti and were introduced to Australia to control these plants.

**Out of Europe**
German wasps like these were introduced from Europe and are now a terrible pest in Australia.

A family recently returned home from a vacation in the Canary Islands and brought back with them an exotic plant as a souvenir. Within a few days, however, scores of greedy termites had begun to emerge from the pot and started to colonize their house. Everything made of wood is now at risk from the greedy insects, particularly since they multiply so rapidly. These pests have even been known to bring whole buildings to the ground. As soon as they are discovered, it will be time to call in the pest controllers. Perhaps that wonderful plant was not such a good idea as a memento after all.

Over the centuries, many species of insects have been introduced to new countries entirely by accident, sometimes with most unfortunate results. One type of tropical cockroach, for example, is said to have been brought to England by Sir Francis Drake and his fleet entirely by accident back in the 16th century. As well as leading the English in sea battles against Spain, Drake was a pirate, and his ships took booty from trading vessels. On one occasion, when the sacks of spices were opened, hundreds of cockroaches poured out and were so quick on their feet that they could not be caught.

**From the east**
The cockroach below, seen crawling all over macaroni, had ancestors that came from the Orient as stowaways among cargo. It is now widespread throughout the world.
▼

Many of the cockroaches in Great Britain today may therefore be direct descendants of those that sailed from the Orient in Drake's ships. Similarly, the American cockroach may originally have traveled on slave ships from Africa back in the 17th century, and the brown-banded cockroach is thought to have been introduced to the United States from a number of islands in the Pacific by soldiers returning home at the end of the Second World War, either in their clothes or in food. It would only take a few to produce millions in less than a year.

**It's the law**
Some countries have very strict regulations about bringing in plants from elsewhere. They may be diseased or infested with unwelcome insects, such as the termites that can be seen emerging from the pot, left. In just a short time they could multiply and cause costly damage.
▼

43

# MAKING TRACKS

Now that the heat of the midday sun has subsided a little, a leopard grasshopper wends its way across the sand, leaving behind it clear evidence that it has passed through this dry environment. The trail made by its six legs will, of course, be of interest to potential predators, for whom this insect will provide a tasty meal if it gets caught.

**Trail-blazer**
Just as we do if we walk on wet mud or on sand, insects will frequently leave tracks behind them as they walk. This highly enlarged illustration of a grasshopper and its trail shows the sort of marks that you may be able to spot. Hunting for insect tracks is not easy, which makes finding some all the more exciting.

**Leaving their mark**
Woodworm beetles have built tunnels in the timbers of a roof, as shown left, but it is their larvae that have done most damage.

As the larva grows, the tracks that it makes in a leaf become progressively wider, too. Some larvae will feed in this way inside rushes or reeds, or in the stems of crops such as corn.

## SECRET FEEDERS

Those insect larvae that feed within plant tissue and eat away at the internal layers of cells usually leave large areas of a plant looking blotchy or white if you hold it up to the light. Sometimes it can be completely see-through in places. While eating, the larvae will have taken in all the healthy green parts of the leaf within which they have been burrowing.

When insect larvae feed in this way, they will rarely be noticed by predators such as birds and so usually survive to adulthood. It is even possible to tell which type of caterpillar or other insect larva was in a leaf-tunnel by the shape of the tracks. All will leave the outside of a stalk or leaf undamaged, however.

If you ever spot holes in the surface of wooden beams or an item of furniture, it is a sure sign of woodworm invasion. Deep inside the timber, and therefore invisible to you, there will be a whole network of tracks that the larvae made as they worked their way along, feeding as they progressed.

Tracks can be left by insects not only on the ground but actually on the inside of leaves by the larvae of small moths or flies. These insects lay their eggs on the leaves; and when a larva hatches, it will bite its way into the leaf and then crawl and feed between the layers. Some of these leaf-miners burrow from the center outward, but others make tracks that wind without a set pattern, just like a meandering river all over the inside of a leaf.

**Telltale signs**
The galleries or tracks that you can see in the photograph of an apple tree leaf, below, have been made by a mining micromoth larva. The leaf has been severely damaged.

**Minute miners**
The meandering trails that are clearly visible inside the leaf, below, have been left by the greedy larvae of leaf-mining insects as they fed within it in the rainforests of Venezuela.

45

# GLOSSARY

**ABDOMEN**
The rear section of an insect's body, containing its digestive and reproductive organs.

**AQUATIC**
Living in water.

**CAMOUFLAGE**
(CAM-OOF-LARJ)
The abitily to blend in with surroundings through color or shape.

**CARNIVORE**
A meat-eater.

**CATERPILLAR**
The larva of a moth or butterfly.

**CHRYSALIS**
(KRIS-AL-ISS)
Another name for a pupa.

**COLONIZE**
To move into an area in large numbers.

**ENTOMOLOGIST**
A scientist who studies insects.

**EQUATOR**
(EK-WAIT-OR)
An imaginary line running horizontally around the middle of the earth.

**FAN DANCE**
A dance performed by bees to ventilate the hive when the temperature gets too high.

**FORAGER**
(FOR-AJ-ER)
A worker bee that goes out to look for a source of nectar.

**FURCULA**
(FUR-KOO-LA)
An organ held by a catch at the rear of a springtail's body. It is released to help this insect spring into the air.

**GRAVITY**
A force that brings something back to earth.

**HALTERES**
(HAL-TERR-AYZ)
Balancing organs.

**HERBIVORE**
A plant-eater.

**HIBERNATION**
(HIGH-BER-NAY-SHUN)
Resting during winter when it is cold and when food is scarce.

**HONEYDEW**
A sweet substance secreted by aphids.

**HOST**
An organism on which a parasite feeds.

**LARVA/plural, LARVAE**
(LAR-VA/LAR-VEYE)
A stage in the life of an insect that goes through complete metamorphosis. It occurs between the egg and the pupal stage.

**MAGGOT**
The legless larva of a true fly.

**MANDIBLES**
An insect's jaws.

**METAMORPHOSIS**
(MET-A-MOR-FOH-SIS)
Takes place when an insect changes from being an egg to an adult. Insects that undergo complete metamorphosis – such as moths and butterflies – change completely. Insects that undergo incomplete metamorphosis – such as cockroaches and dragonflies – look more like the adult as they develop.

**MIGRATION**
Occurs when insects move in large numbers from one region to another.

**NECTAR**
A sugary solution produced by plants. It helps attract insects to flowers so that the insects will pollinate them.

**NYMPH**
(NIMF)
A stage of development between the egg and the adult form in insects such as dragonflies that undergo incomplete metamorphosis.

**PALEONTOLOGIST**
(PAL-EE-ONT-OL-OH-JIST)
A scientist who studies fossils.

**PARALYZED**
Immobilized or prevented from being able to move.

**PARASITE**
A member of a species that feeds off or lives on a member of another species.

**POLLINATE**
To fertilize a plant. The male sex cell, the pollen, is introduced to the female part of a plant, the ovule.

**PROBOSCIS**
(PROB-OS-KIS)
The elongated mouthparts of an insect.

**PROLEGS**
(PROH-LEGS)
Small stumps behind the six main legs of a caterpillar, also called "false legs." They are used for holding onto a surface.

**PUPA/plural, PUPAE**
(PEW-PA/PEW-PEYE)
The stage between the larva and the adult form of insects that undergo complete metamorphosis.

**QUARRY**
The prey of any creature that is predatory.

**QUEEN**
The sole egg-layer in some insect colonies, such as those of bees, wasps, ants, and termites.

**RECTUM**
The last part of the gut.

**RESILIN**
(REZ-ILL-IN)
An elastic substance that helps some insects, such as fleas, leap.

**ROSTRUM**
An extension of the mouthparts of some insects.

**ROUND DANCE**
A dance performed by worker bees to indicate that there is a good source of nectar nearby.

**SPIRACLES**
(SPY-RAK-ELS)
Breathing holes.

**TEGMEN/ plural, TEGMINA**
(TEG-MEN/TEG-MEEN-NAH)
Wing cases.

**THORAX**
The part of an insect's body between the head and the abdomen.

**VENOM**
Poison injected or sprayed by some insects, causing pain, and perhaps paralysis or even death, in other creatures. Humans can have a bad reaction to venom, too.

**WAGGLE DANCE**
A dance performed by bees to indicate that there is nectar to be found. If it was nearer, however, they would do a round dance.

# Set Index

Volume numbers are in **bold**, followed by page numbers.

**A** acrobatics **2**:20 **3**:12,13
aggression **1**:25 **2**:26,27 **5**:28,29; **6**:14,15 see also **fighting**
allergic reactions **2**:39 **5**:21 **6**:15 **7**:22 **8**:23
antennae **1**:22 **2**:12,13,14,16,17, 18,28,29,41,42 **4**:10 **6**:9,19,37 **8**:40
antlions **2**:24 **3**:24 **5**:33 **6**:27,34
ants **1**:14,24,25,31,39 **2**:9,11,19, 33,42 **3**:16,22,23,24 **4**:13,16,17, 18,19,20,21,22,29,44 **5**:8,11,16, 17,33,39 **6**:10,11,14,15,17,21, 28,32,33,37,38,39,40,41 **7**:9,14, 15,16,26,29,30,31,45 **8**:8,17,18, 19,22,23,40 **army 3**:22,23 **6**:15, 32,33 **8**:44,45 **big-headed 6**:14, 15 **bull 5**:30,31 **carpenter 6**:14, 15 **8**:45 **desert 7**:30 **driver 6**:21 **fire 4**:44 **5**:28 **6**:14,15 **harvester 3**:22 **honeypot 4**:18,19 **leaf-cutting 4**:17 **5**:37 **6**:33, 38 **7**:34, 35 **meadow 4**:22 **red 2**:16 **5**:8 **6**:15 **repletes 4**:18,19 **safari 7**:29 **spine-waisted 6**:15 **weaver 1**:24,39 **7**:14,15 **8**:22
aphids **1**:41 **2**:24 **3**:16,17,38 **4**:42 **5**:23 **6**:16,28,40,41 **7**:30 **8**:12, 18,19
aquatic insects **1**:20 **2**:35,41 **3**:9, 14,15,28,29 **4**:29,32,33,36,37 **5**:27 **7**:27 **8**:41
assassin bugs **2**:29 **3**:36,37 **4**:25 **5**:31,33 **8**:24,25,35

**B** bedbugs **2**:18,33 **4**:9 **7**:23
bee-flies **3**:41 **6**:28
bees **1**:15,19,31 **2**:11,26,27,38, 39,42 **3**:11,28,32,38,39 **4**:12,15, 22,29 **5**:11,15,32,33 **6**:13,18,19, 22,23,37,38,39 **7**:21,26,45 **8**:8, 9,10,11,19,23,25,39 **carpenter 7**:11 **drones 1**:19,24,41 **6**:19 **foragers 6**:18,19 **hover 3**:41 **killer 4**:42 **5**:28 **leaf-cutting 3**:10 **7**:34 **longhorned 7**:38 **mason 7**:12,13 **mining 7**:11 **sweat 4**:18,29 **workers 2**:26,27 **6**:18,19,37 see also **bumblebees; dances; hives; honey; honey-bees; nests; queens**
beetles **1**:9,16,17,21,31,34,35 **2**:8,9,10,11,28,32,38,39 **3**:9,11 **4**:12,16, 20,22,26,29,36 **5**:9,30,33,35,40, 45 **6**:13 **7**:21,22,31 **8**:9,27,38, 39,43 **atlas 2**:32 **blister 3**:37 **8**:23 **bombardier 5**:38,39 **burying 1**:36,37 **4**:34 **cardinal 3**:9 **carpet 7**:23 **8**:26 **click 1**:9 **2**:15,31 **3**:12 **5**:40 **cockchafer 1**:17 **2**:42 **3**:25 **Colorado 1**:21 **2**:11 **4**:42,43 **8**:13,19 **darkling 4**:12,26 **5**:39 **7**:10 **death-watch 2**:37 **5**:45 **8**:28,29 **devil's coach-horse 6**:10 **diving 2**:22 **3**:14,15 **5**:15 **dung 4**:34 **5**:36 **elm bark**: 43 **fireflies 1**:8 **2**:14,15 **6**:9 **fungus 1**:37 **furniture 5**:45 **8**:28, 29 **glowworms 2**:15 **4**:41 **6**:9,31 see also **bioluminescence; beetles, fireflies; Goliath 2**:10,11 **5**:9 **ground 4**:16,36 **6**:34,35

Japanese **4**:44 **leaf 1**:34,35 **5**:20 **longhorn 2**:28,29 **4**:20 **5**:9, 24,25 **7**:18,19 **oil 3**:32 **pleasing fungus 4**:24 **rhinoceros 5**:28,36, 37 **rove 3**:28 **5**:29,43 **6**:34 **scarab 4**:26 **sexton 1**:36 **skunk 5**:39 **soldier 6**:44 **Spanishfly 8**:24,45 **stag 1**:16 **2**:27 **3**:27 **5**:28,29 **6**:45 **7**:18 **8**:45 **tiger 3**:34,35 **4**:19,22 **5**:15,31 **6**:10,11 **titan longhorn 5**:11 **tortoise 2**:16 **3**:16 **5**:35 **water 2**:15 **whirligig 4**:32 **wood-boring 1**:44 **3**:27,45; **4**:12,13 **5**:24,25, 44 **7**:18,19 **8**:28,29 see also **ladybugs; weevils**
biggest insects see **size**
bioindicators, insects as **5**:27 **8**:40,41
biological control **3**:42 **5**:30 **8**:43
bioluminescence **1**:8,9 **2**:14,15 **4**:41 **6**:9,34
blood **1**:28,30 **2**:20,28 see also **hemolymph**
bloodsuckers **2**:29 **4**:8,9,10,11, 29,31 **6**:8 **7**:23 **8**:34,35 see also **bedbugs; fleas; flies; mosquitoes, tsetse; parasites**
bugs **1**:35,36,37,41 **5**:33 **6**:40 **7**:21 **cotton stainer 8**:13 **cryptic ambush 2**:36 **cushion scale 2**:24 **flag-footed 1**:9 **kissing 6**:27 **8**:35 **shield 1**:3,36 **squash 5**:39 **stink 1**:37 **5**:39 **8**:17 **thorn 4**:24 **toad 4**:31 **water 7**:27 see also **assassin bugs; bed bugs**
bumblebees **2**:35 **3**:24 **5**:42,43 **6**:16 **7**:41
burrows **4**:22 **7**:9,11 see also **digging; nests; tunneling; underground homes**
bush-crickets **2**:26,41 **4**:31 **6**:27,36,43
butterflies **1**:8,9,27,30,31,44 **2**:6, 11,17,18,19,20,21,24,42,43 **3**:10,11,30,31 **4**:12,15,20,21, 22,24,28,29 **5**:9,15,32,33,35 **6**:16,38,39 **7**:45 **8**:9,38,41,44 **blue-barred morpho 2**:30 **collections 8**:27,38 **clouded yellow 2**:25 **3**:19 **comma 1**:30 **Cramer's blue morpho 1**:8,9 **monarch 3**:18,10 **6**:24 **8**:24,25 **morpho Hercules 1**:32 **painted lady 3**:19 **4**:15 **peacock 1**:44 **5**:35 **6**:30 **purple emperor 4**:20,21 **Queen Alexandra birdwing 5**:11,19 **questionmark 6**:27 **red admiral 3**:19 **two-tailed pasha 1**:31

**C** camouflage **1**:9,30,33 **2**:12, 26,36 **3**:36 **4**:24,30,31 **5**:21,33, 43 **6**:9,26,27 **7**:39,45
cannibalism **1**:18,19,31,39 **4**:40 **5**:21 **6**:42,43
caretakers **6**:40,41
carnivorous plants **5**:33 **6**:28 **7**:26,27
caterpillars **1**:22,26,30,31,32,33, 44 **2**:19,24,25,35,36 **3**:13,18,19, 27,30,45 **4**:14,15,22 **5**:8,22, 23,42 **6**:12,13,16,17,44,45 **7**:10, 16,19,21 **8**:12,13,14,15,18, 19,24,26,27

caves **2**:15,16,17 **4**:40,41
chemical attractants **1**:9 **6**:31,44 **defense 2**:15 **5**:38,39 **markers 6**:38 **signals 6**:14,15,31**
chemoreceptors **2**:42,43 **5**:43
cicadas **1**:11,19,29,42,43 **2**:41,42 **5**:24,40,41 **6**:32 **8**:17,44
circulatory system **2**:13,28,29 see also **blood; hemolymph**
classification of insects **2**:10,11
clean, keeping **2**:17,18 **6**:36,37 **7**:30
climbing insects **3**:16,17
cockroaches **1**:15,21,35 **2**:8,9,11, 18,41 **3**:43 **4**:12,13,16,17,19,40 **5**:8,15,39,41,44 **6**:20,21,45 **7**:22 **8**:30,31,39
cocoons **1**:21,22 **4**:21 **5**:43 **7**:15, 16,17 **8**:14,26
colonies **1**:24 **2**:26,27 **4**:18,19 **6**:18,19,39 **7**:14,15
colonization **2**:21 **3**:42 **4**:42,43, 44,45
coloration **1**:29 **2**:12,20 **most colorful 5**:34,35 **role in display 1**:8,9,17 **6**:44 **warning 1**:33 **2**:13,21 **5**:34,35 **6**:11 **8**:25
compost heaps **4**:16,17
crafty insects **5**:32,33
crickets **1**:10,18 **2**:9,16,17,37,41 **4**:12,22,31,40 **6**:34,35,42,43 **7**:43 **8**:38,39 **cave 2**:16,17 **4**:40 **field 4**:18,22 **Jerusalem 1**:18 **6**:43 **koringkriek 6**:42 **mole 5**:37 **7**:11 **Mormon 1**:19 **tree 2**:37 **wart-biter 4**:22 **weta 4**:23, 44,45 see also **bush-crickets**
cuckoo bees **7**:41 **bumblebees 7**:41 **spit 7**:28,29 **wasps 5**:33 **7**:40,41
cures see **medical treatment**

**D** damselflies **1**:16,17,28,29 **2**:20,21,31 **3**:13 **4**:32 **5**:11
dances **1**:9 **3**:28,29 **6**:18
dangerous insects, the most **5**:20,21
defense mechanisms **1**:17,32,33, 37 **2**:13,28 **5**:39 see also **coloration, warning; self-defense; venom**
definition of an insect **2**:6
deserts **4**:26,27,28,29
destructive insects, the most **5**:44,45 **6**:16,17,22,23
digestive system **2**:13,24,25 **6**:20
digging **2**:15 **3**:24,25 **7**:10,11 see also **tunneling; underground homes**
disease-carrying insects **8**:12, 14,35,36,37,34 see also **bugs, kissing; fleas; flies; pests**
dispersal of insects **4**:44,45
display **1**:8,9,17; **6**:44,45 see also **coloration**
dragonflies **1**:21,29 **2**:8,9,11,20, 21,29,31,45 **3**:10,11,12,13,14, 15,17,29,41 **4**:22,32,33 **5**:11,15, 23,30
drinking **4**:28,29,31 **6**:16,17

**E** earwigs **1**:37 **2**:11 **3**:8,9 **4**:17 **5**:18,19 **6**:37 **7**:30
eating habits **1**:26,31,33,37 **2**:18, 19,24,25,42,43 **3**:17,25,26,27 **4**:14,15,16,17,20,31,34,40 **5**:35,44,45 **6**:16,17,19 see also **cannibalism; digestive system**
edible insects **8**:16,17,20
eggs **1**:16,20,21,22,23,24,25,26, 27,29,34,35,37,38,39,40,41,43 **2**:15,24,33,42 **3**:25,26,27 **4**:8,9, 13,14,15,16,20,21,30,31,33,34, 35,36,37,40 **5**:16,24,26,27,36 **6**:13,14,19,25,33,37,43 **7**:8,11, 12,19,21,24,33,38,39,41,45 **8**:13
excrement **2**:24,25 **4**:34 **6**:34,35
exoskeleton **1**:31 **2**:12,13,18,19, 20,23,44,45 **5**:12,34,35,36 **6**:13, 43
extinct insects **4**:24 **5**:19 see also **fossils; prehistoric insects**
eyes **2**:12,13,18,19,30,31
eyespots **2**:21 **5**:35 **6**:11

**F** families of insects **2**:11
fastest insects see **speed**
feet **2**:42,43 **3**:12,17 see also **legs**
females, deadly **1**:18,19 **5**:21
fighting over **1**:12,13 **2**:23,32
fighting **1**:12,13,19 **2**:23,32 **5**:28, 29 **6**:38,39,45 **7**:41 **8**:38,39 see also **aggression**
fleas **3**:21 **4**:9,10,11 **5**:12,13,15 **7**:28,29,38 **8**:34,35 **chigger 7**:25 **circus 7**:42,43 **human 7**:38 **rat 8**:34,35 **snow 4**:38 **5**:37
flies **1**:12,13,20,21,34,35,44,45 **2**:9,11,15,17,20,21,39,41 **3**:11, 12,33,41 **4**:9,11,13,29,30,31,35, 36,37 **5**:9,32,33,37 **6**:36,42,44, 45 **7**:21,26,27 **8**:8,40 **blackflies 2**:17 **4**:33,36,37 **5**:21 **blowflies 4**:16 **bluebottles 4**:13 **5**:9 **botflies 7**:39 **bumblebee flies 2**:35 **bushflies 4**:29 **caddisflies 7**:13,38 **coffinflies 7**:25 **craneflies 2**:22,24,25 **3**:32 **4**:30,31 **dancefiles 1**:15,17 **4**:31 **6**:43 **droneflies 4**:12 **dungflies 4**:34, 35 **fruitflies 5**:13 **6**:30,31 **gladiator flies 1**:12,13 **greenbottles 8**:9 **hangingflies 6**:44,45 **horseflies 1**:20 **5**:15 **houseflies 1**:21 **2**:10,13,42 **6**:36, 37 **7**:22 **hoverflies 2**:20,30 **3**:8, 41 **6**:37 **8**:8 **lanternflies 6**:8 **marshflies 4**:31 **mayflies 1**:14, 17,29 **4**:33 **5**:26,27 **midges 1**:35 **2**:41 **3**:14 **mosquitoes 1**:14,19, 39,44 **2**:34 **3**:10,33,41 **4**:29, 31,33,39 **5**:9,13,21 **6**:9,43 **7**:39 **8**:36 **parasitic flies 1**:35; **3**:22, 33 **robberflies 1**:19 **4**:22,23 **5**:15, 30,33 **sawflies 1**:23 **6**:12 **scorpionflies 2**:24,25 **4**:20,38, 39 **5**:9,23 **6**:21 **stoneflies 2**:28 **stalk-eyed flies 2**:31 **stilt-legged flies 6**:12 **tsetse flies 1**:34,35 **3**:36 **5**:20,21 **8**:35 see also **gnats; maggots**
flight **2**:15,20,21 **3**:8,9,10,11,12, 13 **4**:45 see also **acrobatics; hovering; wings**
forests **1**:22 **4**:20,21 **7**:45 see also **jungles; woods**
fossils **2**:8,9 **3**:9 **5**:9,27 **8**:39 see also **prehistoric insects**
froghoppers **3**:20 **7**:28,29
fungus **1**:37 **4**:17,20 **gardens 4**:17 **5**:37 **7**:34,35,36,37 **gnats 2**:15 **6**:34**

**G** galls **2**:21 **5**:13 **7**:20,21 **8**:45
gardens, insects in **4**:14,15 **5**:22, 23 **8**:12,13,19 see also **compost heaps; pests; pollination**
gnats **4**:36 **buffalo 5**:21 **fungus 2**:15 **6**:34
grasshoppers **1**:11,17,29,39 **2**:9, 11,17,22,23,24,37,41 **3**:11,20, 21 **5**:32,34,35,39,40 **6**:27 **8**:21, 41 **marsh 4**:31,23 **5**:40 **toad 2**:40 see also **locusts**

47

grasslands **4**:22,23
greediest insects **5**:22,23
grubs **1**:38,39 **2**:33 **3**:25 **4**:43 **5**:20,44 **7**:10,15 **8**:16,17 see also **metamorphosis**
guarding territory **6**:38,39

**H** hairy insects **5**:21,42,43
halteres **2**:21 **3**:12
hearing **1**:10 **2**:6,26,40,41
hemolymph **2**:21,24,27,28,29,45 see also **blood; circulatory system**
hibernation **1**:44,45 **2**:12,38,39 **6**:24,25 see also **overwintering**
hitchhikers **2**:32,33 **4**:45 **7**:35
hives **4**:18 **6**:18,19,22 **8**:10,11
home, insects in the **4**:12,13 **5**:27 **7**:22,23,24,25,43 **8**:26,27,30,31, 32,33
honey **6**:19 **7**:42 **8**:10,11,25
honeybees **1**:15,24,44 **2**:10,11, 21,26,27 **4**:15,29 **5**:8 **6**:18,19, 22,23,33 **7**:42 **8**:8,9,10,11
honeydew **3**:16 **6**:28,40
hopping **3**:20,21 **5**:15
hornets **1**:25,44 **2**:12,13,38 **5**:11,22 **6**:13 **7**:33 **8**:23
hovering **2**:20,21 **3**:11,12,40,41
hunters **1**:18,19, **3**:34,35,36,37, 41 **4**:22,23 **5**:15

**I** insect, definition of **2**:6
insecticides **8**:19,42,43

**J** jaws see **mandibles**
jewelry **2**:9 **8**:38,39
jungle nymphs **4**:24,25
jungles **1**:34,35,43 **2**:23,33 **3**:23 **4**:21,22,24,25 **5**:9,10,34,35 **6**:8, 12,34,38 **7**:19,45 **8**:8

**K** katydids **1**:10 **2**:6,7,17,29,37, 41,44,45 **3**:13 **4**:25 **5**:40 **6**:10,15

**L** lacewings **1**:20 **2**:9 **3**:17 **5**:39 **6**:24 **1**:16,30
ladybugs **1**:17,26,27,38,44,45 **2**:13 **3**:17 **4**:14,15,23 **5**:39 **6**:25 **7**:30 **8**:18,19
largest insects see **size**
larvae **1**:20,21,22,23,24,25,26,27, 32,33,32,38,39,44 **2**:13,24,35 **3**:14,15,17,23,27,34,42,45 **4**:11, 13,22,23,30,31,33 **5**:13,16,23, 31,45 **6**:16,17,33,34 **7**:8,11,14, 15,18,19,20,21,23,41,45 **8**:16, 19,26
leaf insects **5**:16,17 **6**:9,13
leafhoppers **3**:20
leaf-miners **3**:45 **7**:19 **8**:12
leaping **3**:20,21 see also **hopping**
learning from insects **8**:40,41 see also **scientific research**
legs **1**:11,12,19 **2**:12,13,18,19,41, 42 **3**:13,21,30,31 **6**:27
lice **3**:32,33 **4**:8,9,37,39 **5**:13 **7**:23
live birth **1**:34,35
locusts **1**:16,39 **2**:34,35,43 **3**:20 **4**:43 **5**:8,23,31,44,45 **6**:22,23 **8**:12,20,21 desert **1**:39 **2**:45 **4**:29 **6**:17 **8**:20 stink **1**:16 see also **grasshoppers**
longest-lived **1**:24 **5**:24,25

**M** maggots **2**:15,42 **3**:27,33 **4**:9, 13,16 **6**:20 **7**:19,39 **8**:16,38,45
males, and females, differences between **1**:8,9 **2**:6,16,17,21,32, 33 **3**:8,25 **5**:16,17,19,26,29 fighting over **1**:19
mandibles **2**:18,19 **3**:25,35 **5**:21 **6**:14,l5 **1**:16,20

mantises **1**:18,19 **2**:12 **3**:11,12 **5**:32 **6**:29,37 see also **praying mantises**
mating **1**:11,12,13,14,15,16,17, 18,19 **2**:14,15,32,33 **3**:12,13,41 **4**:31 **5**:18,19,26,27,28,40,41 **6**:23,28,29,30,31,38,44,45 flights **1**:14,15,16,17,25 **2**:14,15 **6**:23 see also **nuptial gifts**
medical treatment, using insects for **2**:28,29 **8**:44,45
metamorphosis **1**:28,29,30,31
migration **3**:10,18,19 **6**:23,24,25 **8**:20
mimicry **1**:33 **2**:26 **3**:36 **5**:29,33 **6**:10,11,12,13,32
molting **1**:28,29,43 **2**:23,44,45 **4**:44 **5**:24
moths **1**:22,26,31 **2**:11,15,16,17, 19,32,40,41,42 **3**:22,45 **4**:20 atlas **1**:16 **5**:10,11 black arches **2**:16 buff tip **7**:26 bogong **6**:23 cinnabar **3**:30 clothes **8**:26,27 codlin **7**:19 death's head hawk **3**:10,26 **2**:36 **5**:41 elephant hawk **3**:10,26 emperor **2**:32 giant Agrippa **5**:10,11 hawk moth **8**:13 Hercules **2**:21 hornet **6**:26 hummingbird hawk **3**:40, 41 **5**:14 imperial **6**:26 iron prominent **3**:19 Japanese oak **2**:35 leaf-mining **7**:19 micromoth **3**:45 prominent **6**:26 puss **1**:32,33 red underwing **2**:40 silk **1**:17 **2**:17 **6**:11 **7**:16,17 **8**:14,15 sphynx **3**:33 tiger **2**:42 **5**:42 vampire **6**:8 vaporer **3**:26 **5**:10
mouthparts **2**:8,12,13,18,19,24, 25,42 **3**:36,37 **4**:28 **6**:28,38,43, 44 **8**:24 see also **mandibles; proboscis**
mud **4**:35,35
muscles **2**:22,23,24,27,28,34,35, 37 **3**:9,11 **5**:12,31,36,37,40,41

**N** naming of insects **2**:10,11
nectar **1**:44 **2**:18,24,25 **3**:38,39, 40,41 **4**:14,18,19 **5**:32 **6**:16,28, 38 **8**:8,9,11
nervous system **2**:15,23,26,27, 29,30,42 **5**:12
nests **1**:25 **2**:26,27 **3**:24,25 **4**:34,35 **7**:8,9,10,11,14,15,32, 33,40,41,44,45 see also **colonies; digging; hives; underground homes**
nocturnal insects **2**:40,41 **4**:26 **5**:16,17,43 **6**:8,9
noisiest insects **5**:40,41
numbers of insects **1**:18,34,35,43 **2**:11,12 **4**:21,24 **5**:8,9 **6**:19 **8**:40,41
nuptial gifts **1**:8,15,17 **4**:31,34 **6**:21,30, 31,43,44,45
nurseries, unusual **1**:22,23
nymphs **1**:15,20,27,28,29,36,42, 43 **2**:44,45 **3**:9,17 **5**:16,27,30,31 **6**:17,40 **7**:29 see also **metamorphosis**

**O** oases **4**:28,29
orders of insects **2**:10,11
overwintering **1**:44,45 **3**:18,19 **5**:27 **6**:24 see also **hibernation; migration**

**P** parasites **1**:22,23,35 **3**:9,32, 33 **4**:8,9 **5**:16 **6**:16 **7**:39 see also **bloodsuckers**
parents, good **1**:21,35,36,37 poor **1**:21,34,38,39
parthenogenesis **1**:35,40,41 **2**:33 **6**:41 **7**:21

pests, agricultural **6**:15,28 **8**:12, 13,18,19,42,43 see also **aphids; beetles, Colorado; caterpillars; locusts; scale insects: stick insects; weevils**
pheromones **1**:9,17,24 **2**:26,39, 42 **6**:31,33,44 see also **sexual attractants**
plant-hoppers **6**:8
poisonous insects **5**:34 **6**:11 **8**:24,25 see also **stinging; venom**
pollen **5**:13,42,43 **6**:16,18,19 **7**:11,13 **8**:8,9,10,11
pollination **4**:14,15 **5**:13,32 **6**:28, 29 **8**:8,9,18,19
pond insects **3**:28,29 **4**:32,33 see also **aquatic insects**
pond-skaters **3**:28,29
praying mantises **1**:18,19,39 **2**:19,20 **5**:21,23,30,39 **6**:43
prehistoric insects **2**:8,9 **3**:9 **5**:11 **8**:40 see also **extinct insects; fossils**
proboscis **2**:18,19,25,42,43 **3**:40 **4**:22,40 **5**:41 **6**:8,16,28 **7**:19 **8**:36 see also **mouthparts**
pupae **1**:30,31,44 **2**:34 **3**:14,17, 26 **4**:20,23,33 **5**:16,25 **6**:25 **7**:16, 17 **8**:16 see also **metamorphosis**
pupation **1**:30,31,35 **3**:23 **4**:31 **7**:11,19 **8**:14 see also **pupae**

**Q** queens **1**:19,22,23,24,25,41, 44 **5**:9,17,24 **6**:15,17,19,25,40 ant **2**:33 **3**:23 **5**:24 **6**:15,33 **7**:34 bee **1**:15, 19,24,41 **3**:24 **6**:19,22 bumblebee **3**:24 hornet **1**:25,44 termite **1**:24,25 **5**:16,24 **7**:36 **8**:32 wasp **1**:25,44 **4**:21 **6**:25 **7**:32,33

**R** rare insects **5**:11,18,19,28
recycled homes **7**:12,13
reproductive system see **mating**
resilin **3**:21
resin **2**:8,9
respiratory system **1**:20 **2**:13,34, 35 see also **spiracles**
rock-crawler **4**:39

**S** sap-suckers **1**:27,43 **2**:9,21 **5**:16, 17,45 **6**:8,40,41 see also **aphids; froghoppers; plant-hoppers; scale insects; thrips; treehoppers**
scale insects **3**:27 **5**:16,17 **7**:45 **8**:13
scavenging **4**:12,13,21 **5**:23 **6**:20 **7**:30,31 **8**:18
scent glands **6**:30 patches **2**:17 see also **pheromones**
scientific research **7**:42
self-defense **1**:32,33 **2**:36 **6**:10,11 **8**:22,23 see also **defense mechanisms; stingers; stinging; venom**
sexual attractants **2**:16,42 **6**:30 see also **pheromones**
shared homes **7**:30,31
shortest-lived insects **5**:26,27
silk glands **7**:15,16,17 production **1**:39 **8**:14,15 see also **moths, silk**
silverfish **4**:13,16 **6**:9,33 **7**:24,25
size **1**:11,16,19 **2**:6,8,9,10,21,33, 35,45 **3**:10 **4**:24 **5**:9,10,11,12,13
slow insects see **speed**
smallest insects see **size**
smelliest insects **1**:16 **5**:38,39 **6**:11 see also **bugs, stink; locusts, stink**
snowfield insects **4**:39
social insects **1**:24,37 **5**:8,16 **6**:33 **7**:14,15 see also **ants;**

**bees; termites; wasps**
solitary insects **1**:22 **5**:8,33 **6**:28,29, 37 **7**:40,41,44,45
sound **1**:10,11,17,42 **2**:36,37,38 **4**:22,23,25 **5**:40,41 **6**:31 **8**:28,29 see also **noisiest insects; stridulation**
species, naming of **2**:10,11 new, introduction of **3**:42,43 **4**:42,43
speed **2**:20,21 **3**:9,10,23,26,27, 34,35,40,41 **4**:32 **5**:14,15,16,17
spiracles **2**:34 **3**:15 **5**:41 see also **respiratory system**
springtails **2**:45 **3**:20,21 **4**:31,36, 41 **5**:9 **7**:38
stick insects **1**:27,39,40,41 **2**:11,33 **3**:27 **5**:11,16,38,45 **6**:26,27 **7**:43 **8**:13
stingers **2**:12,38,39 **5**:20 **8**:22,23, 45
stinging **1**:15 **2**:38,39 **3**:22 **5**:28 **6**:11,14,15,21 **8**:22,23
stridulation **3**:10,11,17 **2**:36,37 **6**:14,30 see also **sound**
strongest insects **5**:36,37
swamps **1**:8,9 **4**:4:30,31
swarming **1**:14,15,17,44,45 **3**:18, 19 **4**:29 **5**:26,27 **6**:22,23 **8**:20, 21 see also **mating flights**

**T** taste **2**:18,42,43 **6**:31
teamwork **6**:32,33 **7**:8,9,14,15
temporary homes **7**:28,29
termites **1**:14,15,24,25,29 **2**:11,42 **3**:23,42,43 **5**:11,16,21,24,33,44, 45 **6**:14,23,38,39 **7**:9,36,37,45 **8**:17,32,33,45
thrips **2**:21 **5**:23,45 **6**:43
tracks **3**:44,45 **7**:19
traps **2**:15 **3**:24 **4**:22 **5**:31,33 **6**:34,35
tree houses **7**:44,45
tunneling **1**:22 **3**:24,25,45 **7**:9,11 see also **underground homes**

**U** underground homes **1**:42,43 **3**:22,24,25,35 **4**:18,19 **7**:10,11
urine **4**:28,29 **6**:34 **8**:34

**V** venom **1**:22 **2**:38,39 **3**:36,37 **5**:11,20,21,35,36 **6**:10,11,14,15, 39 **8**:22,23,24,25,44

**W** wasps **1**:22,23,26,27,31,41, 44 **2**:8,11,12,13,26,27,38,39 **3**:11,24,37 **4**:12,14,15,19,22,24, 29 **5**:11,29 **6**:8,10,11,13,16,20, 25,28,29,43 **7**:8,9,20,21,22,23, 32,33,44,45 **8**:9,18,19,23 **fairy fly 2**:21 **5**:12,13 **fig 5**:13 **8**:9 German **3**:42 **5**:21 **6**:37 ichneumon fly **1**:22 **3**:9 **7**:45 mason **7**:10,11 mud **3**:24,25 paper **7**:8,9,16,32,33 parasitic **1**:23,37 Polistes **1**:26,27 potter **4**:34,35 **7**:8 sand **3**:11 **4**:36 spider-hunting **1**:22 **4**:26,27 **5**:30 tarantula hawk **4**:26,27 velvet ants **2**:38,39 **5**:42
weevils **1**:12,23 **2**:23 **4**:12,13 **5**:29,36,44 **7**:8,19,22 **8**:12
wing cases **2**:12,13 **3**:9
wings **1**:8,11,14,15,25,28,29,30, 31,32 **2**:8,12,20,21,29 **3**:8,9,10, 11,12,13,17,40,41 **5**:35 **6**:27,30 **8**:41 see also **flight**
wingspan **2**:21 **5**:10,11,14
woods **4**:20,21 **6**:27 **7**:45 see also **forests; jungles**